SCHOLASTIC

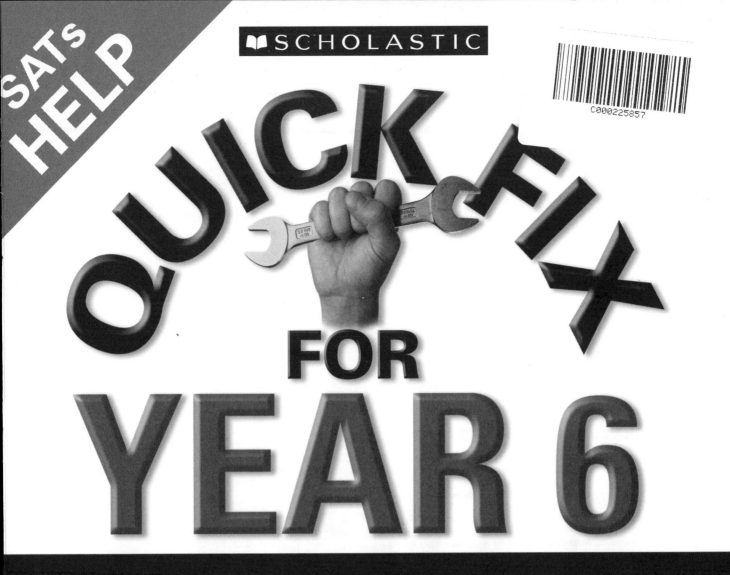

QUICK FIX

FOR

YEAR 6

COMPREHENSION

Stress-busting SATs solutions

Techniques for top marks

Follows the revised PNS Framework

Donna Thomson and Ruth Nixey

CREDITS

Authors
Donna Thomson and Ruth Nixey

Editors
Sarah Snashall, Liz Dalby, Nicola Morgan, Fiona Tomlinson

Series Designer
Anna Oliwa

Designers
Anna Oliwa and Erik Ivens

Illustrations
Garry Davies

Special thanks to
Andrew Vinten, Seb Swana, Jessie and Katie Wood, Alex and Sheila Thomson, Chris and Catherine Parkin and
All the children and staff at Dartington Primary School, S. Devon

Acknowledgements
The publishers gratefully acknowledge permission to reproduce the following copyright material:
Andersen Press Limited for the book cover and extracts from *Wings to Fly* by Patrick Cooper © 2001, Patrick Cooper (2001, Andersen Press Limited). **Richard Edwards** for 'The Word Party' from *The Word Party* by Richard Edwards © 1986, Richard Edwards (1986, Lutterworth/1987, Puffin). **HarperCollins Publishers** for an extract from Chapter 1 of *The Hobbit* by J R R Tolkien © 1937, J R R Tolkien (1937, George Allen & Unwin). **David Higham Associates** for an extract from *The Witches* by Roald Dahl © 1983, Roald Dahl (1983, Jonathan Cape). **The Literary Trustees of Walter de la Mare** and the Society of Authors as their representative for 'The Scarecrow' by Walter de la Mare from *The Complete Poems of Walter de la Mare* © 1969, Walter de la Mare (1969, Faber and Faber) (USA: 1970). **Macmillan Limited** for an extract from Chapter 3 of *The Hitchhikers Guide to the Galaxy* by Douglas Adams © 1979, Douglas Adams (1979, Arthur Baker Limited). **Origin Publishing** for 'Is spring coming early in the UK?' by Alex Kirby from *BBC Wildlife Magazine* April 2006 © 2006, Alex Kirby (BBC Wildlife Magazine) and two extracts 'Copter Camera' and 'Ask the expert' by Michael Kelem from "BBC Focus Magazine" March 2006 © 2006, BBC Focus magazine, www.bbcfocusmagazine.com **Orion Children's Books,** a division of The Orion Publishing Group, for an extract 'Wolf Brother' from *Wolf Brother (Chronicles of Ancient Darkness)* by Michelle Paver © 2004, Michelle Paver, (2004, Orion Children's Books). **Penguin Group Limited** for an extract 'Whirling winds' from *Eyewitness Guides: Weather* edited by John Farndon and Marion Dent © 1990, Dorling Kindersley Ltd (1990, Dorling Kindersley Ltd, London). An extract from *Kasper in the Glitter* by Philip Ridley and illustrated by Chris Riddell © 1994, Philip Ridley (1994, Viking; 1995, Puffin Books). **Chris Riddell** for an illustration from *Kasper in the Glitter* by Philip Ridley © 1994, Chris Riddell (1994, Viking). **Scholastic Children's Books** for an extract 'Montmorency' from *Montmorency* by Eleanor Updale © 2003, Eleanor Updale (2003, Scholastic Children's Books). All rights reserved. **Simon and Schuster Books for Young Readers,** an imprint of Simon & Schuster Children's Publishing Division, for 'Something told the wild geese' by Rachel Field from *Poems* by Rachel Field © 1934, Macmillan Publishing Company; copyright renewed © 1962, Arthur S. Pederson (1934, Macmillan). **Solo Syndication** for 'TV, the only friend for millions of OAPs' by Paul Sims, 'Day the moon took a bite out of the sun' by Ben Quinn and 'Chimps make toddlers look chumps' from "Daily Mail" Thursday, March 30, 2006 © 2006, Daily Mail (2006, Associated Newspapers). **Usborne Publishing Ltd** for an extract 'Anne Frank' from *Usborne Famous Lives: Anne Frank* by Susanna Davidson © 2006, Usborne Publishing Limited (2006, Usborne Publishing Ltd).

Every effort has been made to trace copyright holders for the works reproduced in this book, and the publishers apologise for any inadvertent omissions.

Text © Donna Thomson and Ruth Nixey
© 2007 Scholastic Ltd

Designed using Adobe InDesign

Published by Scholastic Ltd
Villiers House
Clarendon Avenue
Leamington Spa
Warwickshire CV32 5PR
www.scholastic.co.uk

Printed by Bell and Bain Ltd.

1 2 3 4 5 6 7 8 9   7 8 9 0 1 2 3 4 5 6

British Library Cataloguing-in-Publication Data
A catalogue record for this book is available from the British Library.

ISBN 978-0439-94513-4

The rights of Donna Thomson and Ruth Nixey to be identified as the author of this work has been asserted by their in accordance with the Copyright, Designs and Patents Act 1988.

Extracts from The National Literacy Strategy © Crown copyright. Reproduced under the terms of HMSO Guidance Note 8.

CONTENTS

INTRODUCTION

Quick Fix for Year 6 Comprehension is designed to support children and teachers in their preparation for the Year 6 SATs comprehension tasks. It also follows the recommended comprehension strategies in the renewed Primary Framework for literacy.

The activities in this book are designed to teach key comprehension skills across a range of genre and text types.

Each of the 24 lessons is accompanied by one or more photocopiable page to help children develop essential comprehension skills.

Key skills which will enable children to acheive the higher marks in SATs tests are emphasised in each lesson.

The lesson plans are designed to:

■ provide children with texts to stimulate their imaginations;

■ enable children to study examples written by well-known authors;

■ build children's understanding and recognition of how to use the different skills they need to employ to answer literal, inference and evaluation questions;

■ cover key elements that will raise children's marks;

■ focus on the trickier aspects of evaluation and prediction to give children confidence in the test situation.

HOW TO USE THIS BOOK

In order to make the book easy to use, the lessons all follow a similar structure which outlines lesson objectives, lists main points and what to do, and provides a plenary section. These lessons will help teachers to stretch children while building on and reinforcing exsisting knowledge. Extra support is provided for children in the 'Don't panic!' section.

Each lesson can stand alone, although they would be better followed sequentially in order to build on previous learning. The lessons can be included as part of a wider literacy programme, and taught at any time of the school year, as they do not focus on specific NLS termly objectives, but on key aspects that are designed to raise marks in the SATs writing tasks.

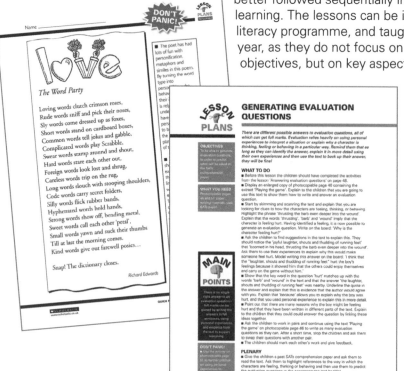

RECIPROCAL READING PROCESS

Following the lessons sequentially will enable the children to build the necessary skills they will need to participate in Reciprocal Reading. Donna Thompson's research into comprehension has proved this is an effective method for teaching reading comprehsion strategies and supports the renewed Primary Framework for literacy. Reciprocal reading involves the pupil as teacher and learner. Within

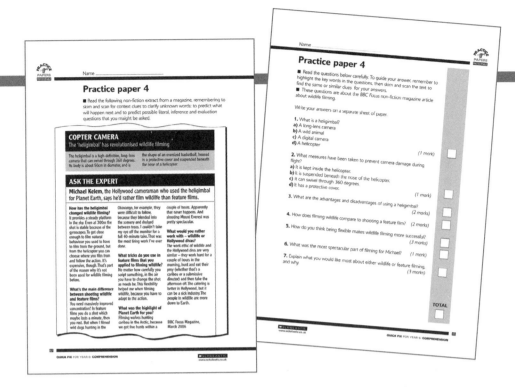

a small mixed-ability group of children (not more than eight) it engages them in collaborative exploration of a variety of texts at different levels; and provides them with a framework for interactive predicting, questioning, summarising and clarifying to support their understanding of text and how the author's intention makes links with their own experiences.

'The teacher supports the student while they practise, giving feedback and additional modelling (guiding) as necessary. Gradually it is intened that the guided practice becomes a dialogue in which groups of students work together with a text, asking questions of one another, commenting on answers, summarising and improving the summary' (The Primary Framework for literacy and mathematics, PNS, DfES, ref: 03855-2006BKT-EN © Crown Copyright 2006)

ASSESSING PUPILS' WORK

Ongoing assessment of pupils work should focus on identifying strengths and areas for improvement. This can be formal or informal, using verbal feedback, children's own feedback or written feedback. Children's comprehension skills will improve when they are clear about what is being assessed. The 'Objective' at the beginning of each lesson plan gives a clear indication of areas for assessment.

Eight sample SATs-style comprehension tasks are included at the end of the book, along with marks and model answers for each. The number of marks for each questions, (as in SATs paper) are an indication of the type of question being asked, for example, 1 mark (literal/easy inference), 2 marks (clarification/complex inference), 3 marks (evaluation). The classification of questions asked in the practice papers are given with the answers in the back of the book.

CRACKING THE CODE

This lesson provides a general introduction to the concepts that follow, and looks at why we read and write, and how we understand what the author is trying to tell us.

WHAT TO DO
■ Ask: 'Why do we read?' Elicit the following answers: to be able to carry out everyday tasks (cooking, reading the TV guide, reading a menu, sending a text message); to be able to communicate with one another; to increase vocabulary; to help with spelling (by recognising familiar word shapes and letter strings); to improve our own writing. Emphasise that reading is an essential skill needed to survive in the world today.
■ Put the children into small mixed-ability groups. Ask them to list the activities they carry out during the day and how the ability to read helps each one. Encourage them to think about what they read while undertaking an activity. After ten minutes, ask to share their ideas.
■ Next, discuss the purpose of writing. Elicit the following ideas: to communicate with a person without speaking to them; to record events and stories and pass them on accurately; to provide information; to entertain; to instruct; to persuade.
■ Explain that you are going to consider the question: 'What is the author's intention?' Explain that when authors write, they have a specific purpose in mind and they carefully select each word and phrase to communicate the intended information to the reader. An author has a picture in their head and their purpose is to give the reader the same picture. To ensure this, they choose words to paint the picture for the reader.
■ Ask: 'What happens when you read? How do you crack the code?' Explain that successful reading is a balance of decoding and comprehending. Decoding relies on understanding how to make sense of symbols and the sounds they make. Explain that good readers do more than just decode the words – they read for meaning. Each word gives the reader an image, like part of a jigsaw and confident readers put these pieces together as they read. They look for the 'who', 'what' and 'where' key words which tell the story. They are keen to find out who is involved, what they are doing and where they are doing it. They realise when they have misread a word because they know that the text doesn't make sense and the picture that forms in their head is nonsense. Good readers will go back and self-correct.
■ Finally, explain that the code has been cracked when the reader understands the message that the author wants to communicate. The picture in the reader's mind is the same as the picture in the author's. Tell the children that the reading and the meaning are best friends – you can't have one without the other.
■ Ask the children to complete photocopiable page 7 where an unsuccessful reader has misread a text and hasn't noticed that the sentence lacked meaning.

PLENARY
■ Tell the children that the SATs comprehension paper gives them an opportunity to show that they have cracked the code of reading and writing. It is their chance to show they understand the author's intention.
■ Explain that there are three levels for understanding a piece of text – literal, inferential and evaluative – and future units will teach them the meaning of each level.

The Hot Seat game

■ Choose one child to answer the questions (below). While asking the questions, show the child the list of answers (below). The child must find the answer then read it and the answer number, aloud in five seconds. If the person in the hot seat cannot answer a question in this time, someone else gets a turn!

Questions

What is said to be found at the end of a rainbow?

What is Britain's highest mountain?

What day do you celebrate getting older?

Which fruit is often put on a stick, covered in toffee and sold at fairgrounds?

What follows doh-ray-mi?

If finders are keepers, what are losers?

What is traditionally eaten on Shrove Tuesday?

In which Italian city is there a famous leaning tower?

Proverbially, how many lives is a cat said to have?

Which vegetable is associated with Halloween?

Which part of Pinocchio's body grew when he told lies?

What is said to be awarded for finishing last in a competition?

How many years is a decade?

What food is mentioned in the rhyme 'This little pig went to market'?

What name is given to slices of bread cut up for dipping into a soft-boiled egg?

Answers

6. Pot of gold	**8.** Ben Nevis	**10.** Birthday	**2.** Apple	**1.** Fa
5. Weepers	**3.** Pancakes	**12.** Pisa	**11.** Nine	**15.** Pumpkin
14. Nose	**4.** Wooden spoon	**7.** Ten	**9.** Roast beef	**13.** Soldiers

Name _____

Skimming and scanning wordsearch

When you skim and scan a text for a word, it's better to have a system. Try going through the text from left to right or top to bottom and say the first letter of the word you are looking for in your head as you search. Try this method as you skim and scan the grid for the following words.

literal	inference	evaluation	author
scan	question	text	skim

Skim

y	j	t	n	k	j	j	a	y	S
i	n	f	e	r	e	n	c	e	K
a	q	u	e	s	t	i	o	n	I
b	m	s	g	h	w	l	e	e	M
t	r	c	t	k	z	i	l	p	I
e	v	a	l	u	a	t	i	o	N
x	w	n	a	s	t	e	o	d	T
t	e	i	o	f	d	r	j	c	N
a	u	t	h	o	r	a	m	q	R
s	h	n	f	y	i	l	a	f	H

Scan

■SCHOLASTIC
www.scholastic.co.uk

Beyond the Deepwoods

The effect was instant. Like a balloon that has been inflated and released, the creature spun wildly through the air with a loud thpthpthpthppppp. Then it exploded, and a mass of small, slimy scraps of yellow and green skin fluttered down to the ground.'

'Yeah!' Twig roared and punched the air. 'I've been and gone and done it! The hover worm is dead.'

As he spoke, dragon's smoke billowed from his mouth. The night had become bitter with an icy north wind. Yet Twig was not cold. Far from it. A glow of pride and excitement warmed his whole body.

'Hel' me,' came a voice from behind him. It sounded strange – as though Gristle was talking while eating.

'It's OK,' said Twig as he pulled himself to his feet. 'I… GRISTLE!' he screamed.

The slaughterer was all but unrecognisable.

Beyond the Deepwoods

■ Read the extract from Beyond the Deepwoods . Find and highlight the following words by skimming and scanning:

slimy	skin	whole	Twig	feet	balloon	excitement

■ Now read the text again and answer the following questions, using complete sentences.

1. Who spun wildly through the air?

_____

2. What happened to the creature before its skin fluttered down to the ground?

_____

3. What was the colour of the creature's skin?

_____

4. Who roared and punched the air?

_____

5. What made the night become so bitter cold?

_____

6. Twig heard a voice. Where was it coming from?

_____

7. Whose voice sounded like it was talking while eating?

_____

8. Who had 'been and gone and done it'?

_____

9. What warmed Twig's whole body?

_____

10. What was like a balloon that had been inflated?

_____

■SCHOLASTIC
www.scholastic.co.uk

Read it and race

■ How quickly can you find and highlight the following words in the text below?

frogspawn	bad	hawthorn	climate	March
food	worried	birds	flowers	vary	early	what
frost-free	late	species	Christmas	

Is spring coming early in the UK?

Is spring coming earlier?
Yes, up to three weeks earlier than in 1975.

Where's the evidence?
Frogspawn usually appears in late February or March. Last year, it was sighted at the end of October – early for 2006, not late for 2005. Bees are not unusual at Christmas. The hawthorn, traditional in late spring, now often flowers in March or April.

What is this doing to wildlife?
It depends on the species, but it can be serious if nature's 'sequence' is upset. For instance, some insects are hatching earlier, but the migrants that eat them still arrive at their normal time. Result: no food for hungry birds.

Should we be worried?
Probably. True, the seasons vary naturally, but it matches what else we know about climate changes. And it isn't just spring. Last year's dry and frost-free autumn kept the trees green in some places until Christmas Eve.

What will happen over time?
There'll be more change. Winter will shrink from both ends – bad news for capercaillies and mountain hares. But other species, such as blackcaps and bumblebees, will benefit because they will be able to find food for a greater duration of the year.

Text © Alex Kirby. BBC Wildlife Magazine, April 2006 Image © David Tipling/Oxford Scientific

INTRODUCING INFERENCE

This unit takes children beyond the literal 'who', 'what' and 'where' questions and adds 'how' and 'why'. These questions can only be answered by inferring things from an image or a piece of text. The analogy of a Text Detective can be used as a device to help children move beyond finding what is 'right there' and delving deeper for evidence to back up what they can infer from a text.

OBJECTIVES
To be able to ask and answer inference questions using a picture.

WHAT YOU NEED
Photocopiable pages 25, 26 and 27; paper and writing materials.

WHAT TO DO
■ Arrange the children in mixed-ability groups of around four. Give each group a copy of photocopiable page 25. Explain that PC Page is in hot pursuit of the men in the foreground. To recap, ask the children what questions he might ask to gather the 'who', 'what', and 'where' information that is right there in the picture. (For example: 'Who is wearing a mask? The man is wearing the mask.'; 'What is PC Page riding? PC Page is riding a bicycle.') Remind the children that these are literal questions.

■ Ask each group to use the picture to generate as many questions and answers as they can. One child from each group should act as scribe and record their questions and answers. Explain that the group who asks the most questions will be the winners.

■ You will notice that the children will quickly and confidently generate lots of literal questions. However, after a short while, they will have asked all of the literal questions that are possible and they will begin (without knowing it) to study the picture at a deeper level and ask inference questions. (For example: 'Is it winter in the picture? It is not winter in the picture because there are leaves on the trees.'; 'Are the owners of the house at home? The owners of the house are probably at home because their car is in the drive.')

■ When you notice that the children are beginning to ask inference questions, stop them and discuss what you have noticed, introducing and explaining the word 'inference'. Ask the children to share some of their questions and answers and decide as a class if they are literal or inference questions.

■ During the discussion, it may be helpful to remind the children that PC Page can only see what is literally 'right there' in front of him and so he is associated with asking and answering literal questions. You could then introduce the Text Detective. She is a higher ranking member of the police force who can solve inference questions by thinking and searching for hidden clues and using them to solve the question. She explains her answers using these clues. She uses the word 'because' to explain how she knows her answer is correct.

■ Explain to the children that they will be asked inference questions as part of their SATs comprehension paper.

MAIN POINTS

Inference questions require you to be a Text Detective to think and search for the clues and solve the answer.

DON'T PANIC!
■ If the children require further practise, use photocopiable page 26 or 27.

PLENARY
■ Ask the children to go through all of the questions they have generated and identify those which are literal and those that are inference. Ask them to explain how they knew which were literal and which were inference. Alternatively, the teams can swap questions, answer them and swap back so that they can be marked.

Every picture tells a story

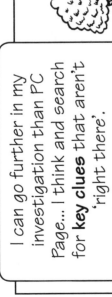

Name _____

Circling clues

■ Look at this picture. Find and circle the clues in the picture that are connected to the words below. Give your reason in the space provided. One has been done as an example.

robber black and white striped shirt, wearing a mask

summer

chase

hidden

stolen

QUICK FIX FOR YEAR 6: COMPREHENSION

Key words as clues

Look carefully at the picture below. What can you see that is literally 'right there' in the picture? Consider further information that may not be obvious at first. Write the key words from the picture that will help you gather more information in the spaces provided. Be a Text Detective... think and search for clues.

DON'T PANIC!

wetsuits		

		surfboards

■ Now write some inference questions and answers on a separate sheet of paper. If it helps, use the question words **Who? What? Where? Why? When?** and the picture key words you have collected. Make sure you have evidence from the picture to back up your answers. For example:

Q. What are the **girls** in the picture? <u>Why</u> do you think that?

A. The girls are **surfers** <u>because</u> they have a **surfboard** each and they are wearing **wetsuits** for going into the water.

SCHOLASTIC
www.scholastic.co.uk

QUICK FIX FOR YEAR 6: COMPREHENSION

UNDERSTANDING INFERENCE

This lesson builds on what children have so far learned about inference to deepen their understanding, and apply it to text. It may help some children if you revisit the characters of PC Page and the Text Detective. Remind them that the Text Detective is of a higher rank than PC Page and can delve deeper to find the answers to inference questions.

WHAT TO DO

■ Display an enlarged copy of photocopiable page 17 (containing the text 'The busy street'). Explain that PC Page has been asked to find out the answer to the following question: 'Has the bus been late before?'. Write the question on the board.

■ Model highlighting the key words in the question ('bus', 'late' and 'before') and begin to skim and scan the text for them. Remind the children that once you have located them the answer will be nearby. After a few moments, explain that there is a problem, and ask if any of the children have spotted what this is. Elicit that none of the key words appear in the text!

■ Explain that to answer inference questions, we need the Text Detective, who thinks and searches for clues to work out the answer from the text. She also gathers evidence to show how she knows the answer.

■ Tell the children that there are inference clues in this text that tell us about a bus. These are the 'key-word clues' and we have to think and search for them. Ask: 'What clues did the author put in to tell us that there was a bus?' Elicit that the answers are 'Number 27' and 'traffic'. Show the children that having found the inference by solving the clue, the answer to the question is nearby; Mrs Jones says that 'it's never on time'. Write the full answer on the board: 'Yes, the bus has been late before. I know this because Mrs Jones says that "it's never on time".'

■ Hand out copies of photocopiable pages 17 and 29, one of each for each pair. Ask the pairs to answer the inference questions. They should record their answers in full and explain how they know. (Answers will vary but will be along these lines: 2. Mrs. Jones was in a grumpy mood because the bus was late again; 3. Mrs. Jones and her son were standing at the bus stop because she was waiting for the bus; 4. Yes, Mrs. Jones was uneasy about the man nearby because she pulled her son closer to her after noticing him hovering nearby; 5. I think an old lady cried out for help because it says she had a shrill voice and because it was a faded pink handbag that had been stolen; 6. No, because it says he was standing nearby in the crowd.)

PLENARY

■ Ask the pairs of children to swap their work and mark each others, giving marks for answering correctly and using complete sentences.

MAIN POINTS

Authors intentionally give their readers extra details by leaving clues for them in the text; this is called inference.
To answer an inference question, you need to look for the clues and solve them.

DON'T PANIC!
■ Use photocopiable page 47 to get children thinking laterally about key word clues they can look for, by experimenting with synonyms.

LESSON PLANS
PHOTOCOPIABLE

Are you a brilliant Text Detective?

Read the extract 'The busy street' before answering the following questions.

Here are some tips for finding clues to answer inference questions.
■ Write down key words from the text to help you answer each question.
■ Write your answer to the question.

The first question has been done as an example.

1. <u>Why</u> was Mrs Jones <u>glancing</u> at the <u>clock impatiently</u>?
Key text words: glanced, clock, impatiently, number 27, time
Answer: Mrs Jones was <u>glancing</u> at the <u>clock impatiently</u> *because* the <u>bus</u> had not arrived on <u>time</u>.

2. What sort of mood was Mrs Jones in? Why do you say that?
Key text words:
Answer:

_____

3. Where were Mrs Jones and her son standing? How do you know that?
Key text words:
Answer:

_____

4. Was Mrs Jones uneasy about the man nearby? How do you know that?
Key text words:
Answer:

_____

5. Who do you think cried out for help? How do you know that?
Key text words:
Answer:

_____

6. Did the figure walk away from the scene of the crime? How do you know that?
Key text words:
Answer:

_____

SKIMMING AND SCANNING FOR SYNONYMS

OBJECTIVES
To be able to identify the key words in a question and search for the corresponding synonyms in the text to find the answer.

WHAT YOU NEED
Photocopiable pages 21, 31 and 47; paper and writing materials.

It would be useful for the children to have completed the lesson 'Understanding inference' on page 28 before doing these activities, which take the skimming and scanning process a step further. Using the work they have already done on identifying key words in questions, they learn to skim and scan quickly for 'key word clues' in the text. This will enable them to answer complicated inference questions quickly, whilst picking up the maximum marks available.

WHAT TO DO
■ Display an enlarged copy of photocopiable page 21, containing the extract from *Beyond the Deepwoods*. Write the following inference question on the board: 'What was odd about Gristle's speech?'
■ Model highlighting the key words 'odd', 'Gristle' and 'speech'. Tell the children that you are now going to skim and scan the text for clues in the form of synonyms, or words that could sensibly replace these key words. Ask the chidlren if they can see any words that mean the same as 'odd' and 'speech'. (Highlight the words 'strange' and 'talking'.) Explain that these are the key-word synonyms and so the answer must be nearby.
■ Write the answer on the board: 'His voice sounded strange; it was as though he was talking while he was eating.' Point out to the children that sometimes the matching words they are searching for in the text, rather than being a substitute word, might relate only in meaning to the words in the question (for example, 'triumphant' and 'punched the air').
■ Hand out photocopiable pages 21 and 31 and ask the children to complete the activities. Remind them to search for synonyms by skimming and scanning the text, saying the words in their heads or looking for words that have similar meanings. Finally, they may try to remember the position of key words or highlight them.
■ After 20 minutes, ask the children to stop and talk through their answers with the class. (Answers: 1. The creature turned round and round because it had been inflated like a balloon and released into the air which had made it spin wildly; 2. Yes, I think that the creature had a slippery body because it says that when it exploded slimy scraps of skin bits landed on the ground; 3. Yes, Twig was triumphant that 'he'd gone and done it' because it says he roared and punched the air; 4. I think that 'dragon's smoke billowed from his mouth' is a good description for the way Twig spoke, because as his warm breath hit the icy cold air it must have looked like thick puffs of smoke coming from his mouth; 5. Yes, Twig was different after he had killed the creature because it says he (the slaughterer) was 'all but unrecognisable'.)

PLENARY
■ Remind the children that the SATs comprehension paper is about proving that they have understood what they have read. Explain that the examiners have asked inference questions which involve the children searching for a synonym to find the answer to see if they understand what the key words in the question actually mean. Their knowledge of vocabulary – or their ability to work out what a difficult word means from reading the rest of the sentence – is being tested.

MAIN POINTS

To answer an inference question, you need to look for the clues (which are often synonyms) and solve them.

DON'T PANIC!
■ For extra practise in finding synonyms, use photocopiable page 47.

Searching for synonyms

Use this sheet with the *Beyond the Deepwoods* extract
on photocopiable page 21.

Skim and scan the text extract to see if
you can find the words that are similar to
those in the box below. You need to think
and search... and skim across and scan
down the text to find the words that have
similar meanings. Look for key words, look
for clues...

immediate _____

blew up _____

turned round and round _____

thumped _____

noisy _____

puffed _____

icy _____

■ Now answer the questions below. Highlight the key-word clues in the questions and
skim and scan the text for similar words to find the answer. Write your answers in full
sentences on a separate sheet of paper.

1. What made the creature turn round and round?

2. Do you think the creature had a slippery body? How do you know that?

3. Was Twig triumphant that he'd 'gone and done it'? How do you know that?

4. Do you think 'dragon's smoke billowed from his mouth' is a good description for the
way Twig spoke?

5. Was Twig different after he had killed the creature? Why do you say that?

UNDERSTANDING COMPLEX INFERENCE

It would be useful for the children to have completed the activities in the lesson 'Understanding inference' on page 28 before undertaking the following lesson. During this lesson the children will learn how to answer another type of inference question, in which the clues are in different parts of the text. This encourages them to search the text more thoroughly for more multi-faceted answers.

OBJECTIVES
To be able to answer complex inference questions.

WHAT YOU NEED
Photocopiable pages 33 and 35; writing materials.

MAIN POINTS

Complex inference questions require the children to find and link clues from different parts of the text. They need to reorganise the information from different sources to form their answer.

DON'T PANIC!
■ If necessary, return to the lessons on 'Understanding inference' (page 28) and 'Skimming and scanning for synonyms' on page 30. For help generating synonyms, use photocopiable page 35.

WHAT TO DO
■ Remind the children that when answering inference questions, it is necessary to find clues left by the author and piece them together. Explain that there are also times when clues that work together will be in completely different parts of the text.

■ Display photocopiable page 33 containing the extract from *Wolf Brother*. Write on the board: 'What did Torak find frightening?' Tell the children that you are going to show them how to answer this complex inference question. Explain that this question would carry two marks if it were in the SATs comprehension paper, and this means there are two pieces of information they must find and put in their answer.

■ Model highlighting the key words from the question 'What', 'Torak' and 'frightening'. Talk about the key words for a moment and show how they can help you to find the clues in the text. For example, as the question is asking for 'what', the answer is likely to be a noun. It is also helpful to remember that as this is an inference question, the word 'frightening' is unlikely to be in the text.

■ Tell the children that you are now going to skim and scan the text for the clues. Ask them if they can see any words that link with the word 'frightening'. First highlight the word 'cry' and point out that nearby it says '…the bear's roars were echoing through the forest.' Therefore it is possible to deduce that Torak is frightened of the bears.

■ Remind the children that the answer needs another piece of information and continue to skim and scan the text. Highlight the words 'heart pounding' and point out that nearby it says 'He saw the blue moonlight through the gaps in his shelter. He saw that the fire was nearly out.'

■ Finally, model linking these clues together to form an answer, such as: 'Torak found the bear's roars frightening. It was also night-time and his fire was nearly out making it dark and cold.'

■ Hand out copies of photocopiable pages 33 and 34 (the extract and related activities). Ask the children to use the techniques you have shown them to complete the activities on the sheet.

■ Answers to these complex inference questions may vary.

PLENARY
■ After 20 minutes, stop the children and talk through the questions and their answers.

■ Ask the children why they think the author chose to write in this way. Why are there inference clues that link up in different parts of the text? Why didn't the author put them all together? One of the possible answers is that it helps to build up and sustain the suspense.

Wolf Brother

Torak woke with a cry.

The last of the bear's roars were echoing through the Forest.

They weren't a dream. They were real.

Torak held his breath. He saw the blue moonlight through the gaps in his shelter.

He saw that the fire was nearly out. He felt his heart pounding.

Again the Forest shook. The trees tensed to listen. But this time Torak realised that the roars were far away: many daywalks to the west. Slowly he breathed out.

At the mouth of the shelter, the cub sat watching him. Its slanted eyes were a strange, dark gold. Amber, thought Torak, remembering the little seal amulet that Fa had worn on a thong around his neck.

He found that oddly reassuring. At least he wasn't alone.

As his heartbeats returned to normal, the pain of his fever came surging back. It crisped his skin. His skull felt ready to burst. He struggled to get more willow bark from his medicine pouch, but dropped it, and couldn't find it again in the half-darkness. He dragged another branch onto the fire, then lay back, gasping.

Text © Michelle Paver

Questions based on the extract from *Wolf Brother*

■ Read the *Wolf Brother* extract carefully.

■ Before attempting to answer the questions below, try highlighting the key words in them. Use these key words to help you search for clues in the text.

■ Answer the questions in full. You can use parts of the questions to guide your answers. There are two marks for each question.

1. Was Torak frightened? Explain how you know that.

_____

_____

2. Do you think that Torak was in immediate danger? How do you know that?

_____

_____

3. What made Torak feel less fearful? Why do you say that?

_____

_____

4. Do you think Torak had been ill for some time? How do you know that?

_____

_____

5. Do you think Torak lives in the present day? Why do you say that?

_____

_____

Words with similar meanings

> The slippery mud oozed between their fingers as the two squelching figures scrambled up the steep bank.
>
> "Quick – the hedge," panted Charlie, heaving the loot into the ditch with him. "I can 'ear them coming."
>
> A distant siren sliced through the stillness of the warm day and, beyond the nearby hill, an intermittent squeaking and rattling warned the pair that the long arm of the law might snatch them up at any minute.

■ Choose two words from the text and write them in the middle of each blank web. Write words that have similar meanings in the spaces. How many can you find?

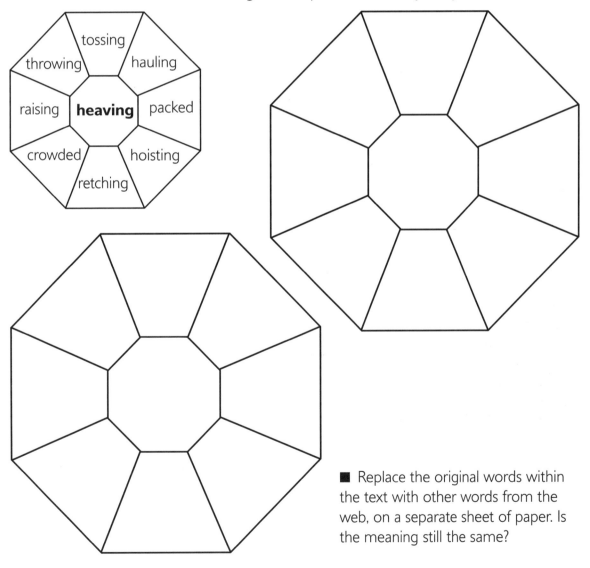

■ Replace the original words within the text with other words from the web, on a separate sheet of paper. Is the meaning still the same?

GENERATING INFERENCE QUESTIONS

It is vital that the children can see how easy it is to ask and answer inference questions. This lesson teaches them to predict inference questions based around inference they can identify in the text. Being able to predict the questions as they are reading is an excellent exam technique and it will enable the children to answer the questions more quickly, filling them with confidence.

WHAT TO DO

■ It would be useful for the children to have completed the activities in the lesson 'Understanding inference' on page 28 before tackling this lesson.

■ Remind the children that authors intentionally tell their readers extra details by leaving subtle clues for them in the text and that this is called inference.

■ Display photocopiable page 37 containing the extract 'The Getaway'. Read the text through once and explain that you are going to use it to model writing an inference question of the kind that the children will see on the SATs comprehension paper.

■ Start by slowly skimming and scanning the text and explain that you are looking for subtle inference clues the author has left that give you additional information without having to put it literally 'right there'.

■ Highlight the phrase 'The slippery mud oozed between their fingers…' and tell the children that this phrase contains inference. It tells us many other pieces of information without having to literally say each one.

■ Ask the children if they can give you any examples of what the phrase tells them. Answers should include: the mud is very wet; perhaps it has been raining or that the river running under the bank is deep; the men had dirty hands after climbing up the bank.

■ Explain that you will use one of these possible answers to write your inference question. Write on the board 'Were the men's hands dirty after climbing the bank? How do you know that?' Ask a child to write the answer underneath, as a full sentence, such as 'Yes, the men's hands were dirty after they had climbed the bank because the mud had "oozed between their fingers".'

■ Point out to the children that the key words from the question are also in the answer. Explain that it is also a good idea to quote from the text as it will allow the children the opportunity to provide clear, concise evidence to back up their answer.

■ Ask the children to work in pairs. Hand out a copy of photocopiable page 37 and ask them to continue using 'The Getaway' to create as many inference questions as they can on another sheet of paper. After a short time, stop the children and ask them to swap their questions with another pair or team. They should then answer the inference questions they have been given.

PLENARY

■ Ask the children to mark each other's work and give feedback. They should comment on whether full sentences were used, if the answers were backed up with evidence from the text and also on spelling and punctuation.

The Getaway

The slippery mud oozed between their fingers as the two squelching figures scrambled up the steep bank.

"Quick – the hedge," panted Charlie, heaving the loot into the ditch with him. "I can 'ear them coming."

A distant siren sliced through the stillness of the warm day and, beyond the nearby hill, an intermittent squeaking and rattling warned the pair that the long arm of the law might snatch them up at any minute.

LITERAL AND INFERENTIAL INTENTION IN FICTION

OBJECTIVES
To be able to locate examples of literal and inferential intention within a text, and explain the difference between them.

WHAT YOU NEED
Photocopiable pages 14, 23 and 39; paper and writing materials; past SATs papers.

MAIN POINTS
If you understand the kind of question you are being asked, it will be easier and quicker to find the answer.

DON'T PANIC!
■ To recap on generating literal questions from text, return to the 'person, action, place' game on photocopiable page 14.
■ To practise skimming and scanning, try a variation of 'Read it and race' (on photocopiable page 23) using a past SATs comprehension paper.

It is important that the children can see how easy it is to identify question types. After they have read the text in a SATs comprehension paper, they will be amazed when they are able to say which questions are literal and which are inference. It is a great exam technique that will enable them to answer questions more quickly. They will instantly know if they should skim and scan the text for the same key word as in the question (literal question) or a different word/clue that has similar meaning (inference question).

WHAT TO DO
■ Remind the children that the literal intention of a text is to communicate information by putting it 'right there' in the text. (You could remind them of the phrase 'Who? What? Where? It's literally 'right there'!')
■ Now remind the children that the inferential intention of a text is to communicate extra details. These take the form of subtle clues that authors leave for their readers to solve.
■ Display photocopiable page 39 containing the extract from *Montmorency*. Read the text together.
■ Explain to the children that a good test to see if they really understand the author's literal and inferential intention is to find out if they can tell the difference between them. Tell them that they are going to do this by using all of the information they can find in the text to write questions, and that you will first show them how.
■ Underline the first sentence of the extract. Ask the children to suggest literal questions they could ask about this sentence. Remind them to look for key words to help them form the questions, which could include: 'Whose cab clattered towards Covent Garden?'; 'Where did Montmorency's cab clatter towards?'; 'What month of the year is it?'; 'What time of day is it?'
■ Now ask them to suggest some inference questions. Remind them to look for subtle clues in the text, and to use these to generate their questions. Questions could include: 'Has it been a warm day? How do you know that?'; 'What was the surface of the street like? How do you know that?' (You may need to remind the children that literal questions usually begin with the words who, what and where.)
■ Ask the children to work in pairs and give each pair a copy of photocopiable page 39. They should continue to go through the rest of the text, deciding if the information is literal or inferential and writing the appropriate questions on a separate sheet of paper.
■ After 15 minutes, stop the children and ask them to swap their questions with another pair. They should then answer the literal and inference questions they have been given.

PLENARY
■ Ask the children to take back their original questions, to mark each other's work and give feedback. They should comment on whether full sentences were used, if the answers were backed up with evidence from the text and also on spelling and punctuation.

MONTMORENCY

Montmorency's cab clattered towards Covent Garden as the cool sunlight of the early May day began to give way to evening. The shops were closed and the streets were quiet, until, as they turned from the Strand into Bow Street, they hit a traffic jam of carriages dropping off the rest of the audience. Montmorency had left himself plenty of time, unsure of how long it would take him to find his seat, but plenty of others seemed to have had the same idea. He decided to get out and walk the short distance to the Opera House. He stayed well to the side of the road and stepped carefully. The press of horses had deposited piles of dung here and there, and as carriage doors swung open he had to take care not to be hit, or have his new hat knocked into the dusty road. Two familiar figures were leaning against a wall, shouting saucy comments to the crowd. He was about to smile at Mrs Evans and Vi when he remembered who he was.

Text © Eleanor Updale

LESSON PLANS

LITERAL AND INFERENTIAL INTENTION IN NON-FICTION

It is very likely that the children will be faced with a non-fiction text of some kind in their SATs comprehension paper. (See practice papers 4 and 5.) It is vital for the children to understand that they will be asked the same types of questions with non-fiction texts as with fiction. Tell them not to simply expect literal questions on non-fiction pieces – there will be inference and evaluation ones too. (For evaluation questions see pages 42–51.)

OBJECTIVES
To understand the literal and inferential intentions of non-fiction authors, and to understand the purpose of inference in non-fiction (to add interest and to persuade).

WHAT YOU NEED
Photocopiable pages 41 and 51; paper and writing materials.

MAIN POINTS

Be prepared to tackle non-fiction!
Non-fiction contains literal information, inference and evaluation just as fiction does.

DON'T PANIC!
■ Use photocopiable page 51 for more practise with similes and metaphors.

WHAT TO DO
■ Ask the children to suggest all the types of non-fiction texts they can think of. Write their answers in a list on the board, for example: recipe, newspaper/magazine, letter, recount, leaflet, advert, obituary, information text.
■ Next ask the children to discuss what they think the purpose of each of the non-fiction text types listed is, and write down their findings. For example, the purpose of a recipe is to instruct; the purpose of a tabloid newspaper is to inform and recount. Draw their attention to how the purpose of non-fiction text varies depending on what type of text it is.
■ Ask the children if they think that the purpose of a non-fiction text changes the way the authors write. Ask if authors of non-fiction have to write only in a literal way just because they are presenting facts, or is it possible to have inference in non-fiction? They should agree that non-fiction can include inference. (See the lesson 'Fact, opinion and evaluation in non-fiction' on page 52 for further work on non-fiction in newspapers.)
■ Explain that authors of non-fiction texts like to enhance the information with extra details in the form of 'clues' (inference) to make the facts more interesting for the reader. They may use similes and metaphors for this purpose.
■ Explain that writers of non-fiction may also use inference to influence their readers' opinions. For example, a journalist may include hidden inference in what seems to be a purely factual news story to push a particular point of view or to persuade the reader, without appearing to do so.
■ Display an enlarged copy of photocopiable page 41 and read the two extracts together. Explain that they are non-fiction texts and ask the children to suggest what their purpose is. (To inform and explain.)
■ Hand out photocopiable page 41 to pairs of children. Ask the pairs to re-read the texts and work together to highlight the literal words and phrases in one colour and the inference words and phrases in another. Remind them that inferential information may be in the form of a simile or metaphor. Encourage them to discuss and justify their decisions.

PLENARY
■ Ask the children if they noticed differences in the way the two pieces were written. They should have discovered that the author of 'Life in Tudor Times' presented the facts in a very literal way, while the author of 'Whirling Winds' presented the facts with some use of inference. Discuss the effect this has on the reader in each case, and the purpose of each text.

Life in Tudor Times

The current population of England and Wales is approximately 53 million, however in Tudor times the population was far lower. At the start of the Tudor period there were about 2.3 million people, increasing to about 3 million people when Elizabeth was growing up. Three quarters of the population lived in the countryside, with everyone else living in London or one of a few small towns.

Illness and death were common events in most homes because the Tudors had limited medical knowledge and only basic medicines. Many babies died and those who did live then had to survive frequent outbreaks of serious illness, such as smallpox and the plague.

Tudor teachers used to whip their students with canes, leather straps or birch twigs because they thought pain was good for them.

Text © 2007. Scholastic Ltd

Whirling Winds

TORNADOES GO BY MANY NAMES – twisters, whirlwinds, and more. Wherever they strike, these whirling spirals of wind leave a trail of unbelievable destruction. They roar past in just a few minutes, tossing people, cars, and strong buildings high into the air, then smashing them to the ground. Meteorological instruments rarely survive to tell what conditions are really like in a tornado. Winds probably race around the outside at over 400 kph (240 mph), while pressure at the centre plunges several hundred millibars lower than outside. This creates a kind of funnel or vortex that acts like a giant vacuum cleaner sucking things into the air, tearing the tops off trees, and blowing out windows. Tornadoes hang down like an elephant's trunk from giant thunderclouds, and may strike wherever thunderstorms occur.

Text © 1990, Dorling Kindersley Ltd Image © 1998 Corbis Corporation

INTRODUCING EVALUATION

This lesson focuses on how to answer evaluation questions, using visual imagery as a starting point. It builds upon what the children already know about literal and inference questions, and encourages them to add their own experiences into the mix in order to answer 'why?' questions. It also reinforces the idea that all kinds of questions must be backed up by evidence in the source material.

OBJECTIVES
To understand that an evaluation question asks you to think about a character's feelings or actions using your literal and inference skills and personal experiences to answer.

WHAT YOU NEED
Photocopiable page 43; writing materials.

WHAT TO DO
■ Tell the children that they are going to look at another kind of question in this lesson, but first they are going to play a game to recap their knowledge of inference questions.

■ Divide the class into mixed-ability groups of around four and give each team a copy of photocopiable page 43. Ask each team to choose a scribe to record their questions. Give the children a minute or so to familiarise themselves with the picture.

■ Challenge the teams to generate as many inference questions as they can from the picture. Remind them to take a closer look at the picture to see clues the artist has left that show additional details. For example, some of the children are wearing shorts and T-shirts and this tells us that it is perhaps early summer.

■ After five minutes, ask the teams to swap their questions. Encourage the teams to look carefully at the inference questions they have been given. Are any of them about the characters' thoughts, feelings or behaviour? Would any of the questions require the children to think about their own experiences to answer them, and not just the clues in the picture?

■ Ask children to volunteer examples. If any questions do rely on personal experience or relate to thoughts, feelings or behaviour, explain to the children that these are evaluation questions.

■ Use an example to draw out the difference between inference and evaluation. Look at the boy in the picture. He is frowning and sitting on his own and from this we can infer that he is sad. But explain that the inference clues can't tell us why he is sad.

■ Tell the children that we can use evaluation (our own personal experiences) to suggest why he is feeling sad, and we can use the picture to back up our ideas. Ask for suggestions: he might have been caught out; he might have had an argument; he might be feeling unwell; he might want to play football or his friends might be ignoring him – we all know what these feel like. Explain that we must also make sure that the artist or author would agree – it would be silly to say that the boy is feeling sad about England losing in the World Cup as there is no way of backing that up.

PLENARY
■ As a whole class, look at the other characters in the picture and identify what they are thinking and the way they are feeling or behaving. Together, generate evaluation questions that ask why they are thinking/feeling/ behaving this way and ask the children to use their own experiences, which can be backed up with evidence from the picture, to explain why. Discuss the answers to these evaluation questions.

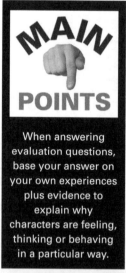

When answering evaluation questions, base your answer on your own experiences plus evidence to explain why characters are feeling, thinking or behaving in a particular way.

DON'T PANIC!
■ It may be helpful to recap on literal and inference questions using the characters of PC Page and the Text Detective (see pages 10–17 and 24–29).

Every picture tells a story

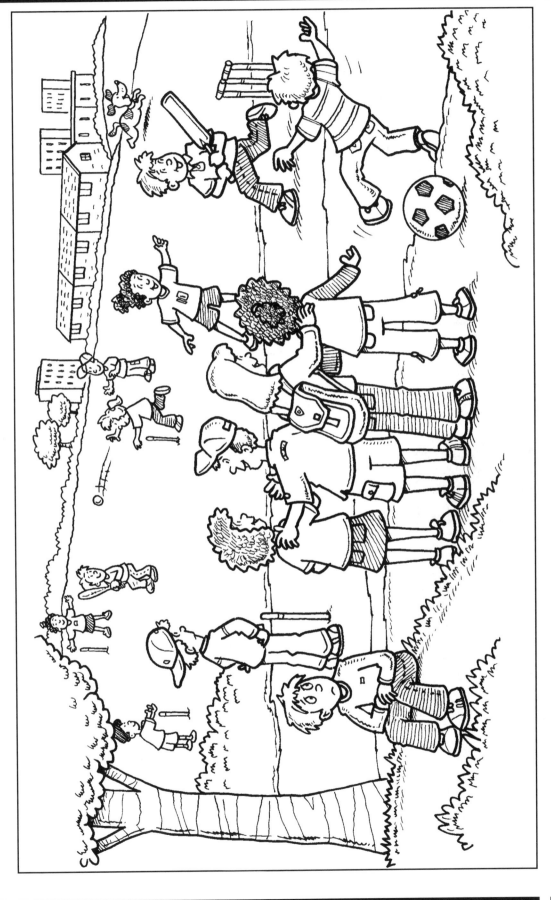

UNDERSTANDING EVALUATION

This lesson focuses on evaluating a text, by first using personal experience to generate reasons why characters act, think or feel in a particular way, then referring back to the text to decide on the most sensible answer, based on evidence.

OBJECTIVES

To understand how to find the answer to an evaluation question and back it up with evidence in the text.

WHAT YOU NEED

Photocopiable pages 19, 45, 46 and 47; wirting materials.

Find reasons for actions, thoughts or feelings using your experience and evidence in the text.

DON'T PANIC!

■ For a direct comparison between literal, inference and evaluation questions using a previous text, use the main activity from lesson 'Answering literal questions (page 16).

■ For a slightly easier text, or for more practise finding actions, thoughts and feelings, use photocopiable page 46.

■ Use photocopiable page 47 to help the children identify emotions from words in the text.

WHAT TO DO

■ It would be helpful for the children to have completed the activities in the lesson 'Introducing evaluation' (page 42) before doing this lesson.

■ Display an enlarged copy of photocopiable page 45 'The Scarecrow' by Walter de la Mare and read the text.

■ Remind the children that evaluation is simply using your own experiences to explain characters' thoughts and feelings.

■ Return to the text and ask the children to identify all of the actions, thoughts and feelings in the text. List them on the board under these three headings. For example:'scan' (action), 'strange' (thought) and 'rapture' (feeling).

■ Next, ask the children to suggest as many reasons as they can for each action, thought or feeling on the list. Start with the example, reasons to 'bow my head': to show respect; against snow or rain; to agree with someone; in sadness. The children could use their personal experiences to create a very long list!

■ Refocus the children's attention on the text. They will soon realise that the only reason they can use to explain why this character is bowing his or her head is because of the bad weather. The children are likely to have been caught in rain, wind and snow themselves at some time and so will be able to explain in detail why the character is doing this – perhaps to keep the rain and snow out of his eyes, or to huddle deeper into a hood or stay under an umbrella.

■ Hand out copies of the poem to pairs of children, and ask them to work together to highlight words and phrases that describe personal feelings, thoughts and actions that they can recognise from their own experiences. Encourage them to consider how it makes them feel. Can they identify with the character in this poem in any way? Have they experienced any of these feelings or done any of the things the character talks of?

■ Ask the children to list the actions, thoughts and feelings that they have identified in one narrow column, and to write down reasons for each one a wide second column, exploring each word or phrase as fully as possible. They should back up their reasons using evidence in the text, and write them out using full sentences. Remind them to draw their answers from their own experience, but also to reflect what the author might have intended.

PLENARY

■ Discuss the children's findings as a class. Ask them to share their reasons for the actions, thoughts and feelings of the character in the text. Pay particular attention to how they used their own personal experiences to help them answer.

The Scarecrow

All winter through I bow my head
   Beneath the driving rain;
The North Wind powders me with snow
   And blows me black again;
At midnight in a maze of stars
   I flame with glittering rime,
And stand, above the stubble, stiff
   As mail at morning-prime.
But when that child, called Spring, and all
   His host of children, come,
Scattering their buds and dew upon
   These acres of my home,
Some rapture in my rags awakes;
   I lift void eyes and scan
The skies for crows, those ravening foes,
   Of my strange master, man.
I watch him striding lank behind
   His clashing team, and know
Soon will the wheat swish body high
   Where once lay sterile snow;
Soon shall I gaze across a sea
   Of sun-begotten grain,
Which my unflinching watch hath sealed
   For harvest once again.

Walter de la Mare

Name _____

Playing the game

■ Read the story extract and highlight the words that you think describe the characters' actions, thoughts and feelings. Use a different colour for each.

The joyful laughter, shouts and thudding of running feet boomed in his head, thrusting the barb even deeper into the wound. He didn't care that the wetness of the dewy grass was seeping through his tracksuit bottoms. No one would notice when he stood up anyway. He swallowed hard as the tears stung his eyes. He could bowl a ball with the best of them. Joe wasn't the only one.

A group of friends shoving and poking each other playfully, assembled close by to watch the game. He looked up and squeezed out a smile, but no one responded. Defeated, he stiffened his back and turned his head away. Nobody cared about him. Wiping the tears away with the back of his hand, he lunged forward and angrily ripped and tore at the clumps of damp grass.

"What are you doing over here?" chirped a familiar voice behind him.

Word webs

■ Authors choose words carefully to enable you to better understand what is happening in a piece of text. What happens when you replace a word they have used? Does it increase the amount of information or reduce it?

■ Use these word webs to generate similar words to replace a word in a piece of text. Write the original word in the middle of the web and fill in similar words around the outside.

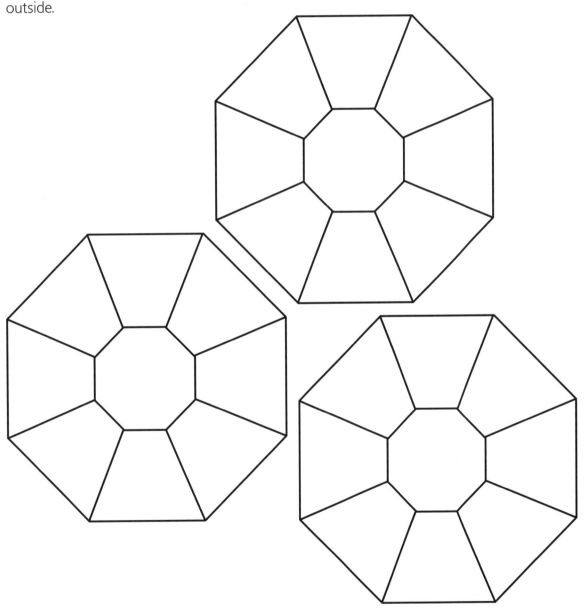

■ Now replace the original word in each sentence with other words from the web, using a separate sheet of paper. Is the meaning still the same?

QUICK FIX FOR YEAR 6: COMPREHENSION

LESSON PLANS

ANSWERING EVALUATION QUESTIONS

This lesson explores evaluation questions further, and gives the children a technique to use to answer these types of questions fully, in order to pick up all the marks available.

OBJECTIVES
To know how to answer an evaluation question.

WHAT YOU NEED
Photocopiable pages 47 and 49; wirting materials.

WHAT TO DO

■ Display an enlarged copy of the extract on photocopiable page 49, and read it together. Ask the children what they know about Anne Frank and the situation in Germany at the time of World War II. If necessary, provide the children with some simple background information.

■ Ask the children to work in pairs and imagine that they have been given the opportunity to interview Anne Frank. Allow them ten minutes to prepare interview questions based on the text. For example: 'What do you mean when you say "a deathly oppressive silence hangs over the house"?' 'Why do you "feel like a songbird whose wings have been ripped off"?'

■ The children take it in turns to ask each other their questions and answer as if they were Anne Frank. They should answer as fully as they can, using their personal experiences to help them to explain in more detail.

■ Explain to the children that they will be asked these kind of evaluation questions (about the reasons for characters' actions, thoughts and feelings) in the SATs comprehension paper. Point out that these are usually easy to recognise as they often begin with 'Why do you think…', 'How do you think…' or 'What do you think…'.

■ Tell the children that evaluation questions are usually worth three marks. Explain that you are going to show them how to answer to achieve full marks. Write the following on the board: 'How do you think Anne felt about the house she was living in? Why do you say that?'

■ First, identify how Anne felt about the house. Remind the children to use the key words in the question – 'felt' and 'house'. Model skimming and scanning the text for these words and highlight them. Point out the lines 'the house clings to me as if it were going to drag me into the deepest regions of the underworld' and 'feel like a songbird whose wings have been ripped off'. The children should deduce that Anne felt depressed, bored, trapped and frustrated.

■ To achieve the other marks the children need to explain why Anne is feeling this way. They should use their own experiences to explain why and quote from the text to provide evidence. For example: 'I think that Anne felt depressed living in the house because she talks about the silence being '"deathly" and "oppressive". I think she feels bored because she talks of wandering "from room to room" and she feels frustrated "like a wingless songbird in a cage". I think she must feel like a prisoner who is locked up in her own home, that there is no escape and that she has no future ahead of her.'

■ Hand out photocopiable page 49 and ask the children to work individually to answer the other evaluation questions.

■ Answers may vary but must relate to the text.

PLENARY

■ After 15–20 minutes, stop the children and talk through some of the questions and answers. Encourage the children to assess the success of the answers, and suggest how many marks each would be awarded in the context of the SATs comprehension paper.

MAIN POINTS

Evaluation questions usually begin with phrases like 'What do you think…' and are often worth 3 marks, 1 mark for each separate point you make.

DON'T PANIC!
■ Try looking at photocopiable page 47 for help in identifying emotions.

Anne Frank

"The atmosphere is stifling, sluggish, leaden," she wrote. "A deathly oppressive silence hangs over the house and clings to me as if it were going to drag me into the deepest regions of the underworld! …I wander from room to room, climb up and down the stairs and feel like a songbird whose wings have been ripped off and who keeps hurling itself against the bars of its dark cage."

One night, Anne dreamed of Lies. She was dressed in rags, her face thin and worn. She looked at Anne with such sadness in her eyes. "Help me," she seemed to say, "rescue me from this hell!"

"But I can't help you!" Anne called out. "I can only stand by and watch while you and other Jews suffer and die." When Anne woke, she was crying. "What's happened to Lies?" she thought. "She's probably been taken away to the camps. Why have I been chosen to live, while she's probably going to die?"

For days after, Anne kept seeing those enormous eyes. They haunted her. She longed to talk to someone… "Daddy's the only one who understands me," she wrote.

Text © Susanna Davidson

■ Answer the following evaluation questions. Remember they are usually worth 3 marks.

Why do you think Anne felt safe from the probable fate of her friend Lies?

_____

Why do you think Anne doesn't expect Lies to survive?

_____

Do you think Anne was living alone in the house?

_____

Was Anne free to leave the house?

_____

Why do you think Anne wrote about her time in the house?

_____

GENERATING EVALUATION QUESTIONS

There are different possible answers to evaluation questions, all of which can get full marks. Evaluation relies heavily on using personal experiences to interpret a situation or explain why a character is thinking, feeling or behaving in a particular way. Remind them that as long as they can identify the answer, explain it in more detail using their own experiences and then use the text to back up their answer, they will be fine!

WHAT TO DO
■ Before this lesson the children should have completed the activities from the lesson 'Answering evaluation questions' on page 48.
■ Display an enlarged copy of photocopiable page 46 containing the extract 'Playing the game'. Explain to the children that you are going to use this text to show them how to write and answer an evaluation question.
■ Start by skimming and scanning the text and explain that you are looking for clues to how the characters are feeling, thinking, or behaving. Highlight the phrase 'thrusting the barb even deeper into the wound'. Explain that the words 'thrusting', 'barb' and 'wound' imply that the character is feeling hurt. Having identified a feeling, it is now possible to generate an evaluation question. Write on the board: 'Why is the character feeling hurt?'
■ Ask the children to find suggestions in the text to explain this. They should notice the 'joyful laughter, shouts and thudding of running feet' that 'boomed in his head, thrusting the barb even deeper into the wound'. Ask them to use their experiences to explain why this would make someone feel hurt. Model writing this answer on the board: 'I think that the "laughter, shouts and thudding of running feet" hurt the boy's feelings because it showed him that the others could enjoy themselves and carry on the game without him.'
■ Show that the key word in the question 'hurt' matches up with the words 'barb' and 'wound' in the text and that the answer 'the laughter, shouts and thudding of running feet' was nearby. Underline the quote in the answer and explain that this is evidence that the author would agree with you. Explain that 'because' allows you to explain why the boy was hurt, and that you used personal experience to explain this in more detail.
■ Point out that there are many reasons why the boy might be feeling hurt and that they have been written in different parts of the text. Explain to the children that they could could answer the question by linking these ideas together.
■ Ask the children to work in pairs and continue using the text 'Playing the game' on photocopiable page 46 to write as many evaluation questions as they can. After a short time, stop the children and ask them to swap their questions with another pair.
■ The children should mark each other's work and give feedback.

PLENARY
■ Give the children a past SATs comprehension paper and ask them to read the text. Ask them to highlight references to the way in which the characters are feeling, thinking or behaving and then use them to predict the evaluation questions in the accompanying test booklet.

The Word Party

Loving words clutch crimson roses,
Rude words sniff and pick their noses,
Sly words come dressed up as foxes,
Short words stand on cardboard boxes,
Common words tell jokes and gabble,
Complicated words play Scrabble,
Swear words stamp around and shout,
Hard words stare each other out,
Foreign words look lost and shrug,
Careless words trip on the rug,
Long words slouch with stooping shoulders,
Code words carry secret folders,
Silly words flick rubber bands,
Hyphenated words hold hands,
Strong words show off, bending metal,
Sweet words call each other 'petal',
Small words yawn and suck their thumbs
Till at last the morning comes.
Kind words give out farewell posies…

Snap! The dictionary closes.

Richard Edwards

■ The poet has had lots of fun with personification, metaphors and similes in this poem. By turning the word type into personalities who behave according to their identity the poet is relying on the understanding we have from our personal experience to be able to enjoy the joke he has planted in each line of the poem.

■ On a separate sheet of paper explain why you think the words in each line are associated with each other. For example: 'Loving words clutch crimson roses: Crimson roses are what people give to someone they love. If somebody clutches something it suggests they are holding it close as if they are scared of dropping it; as they would be if they were going to give it to someone they loved.'

FACT, OPINION AND EVALUATION IN NON-FICTION

OBJECTIVES
To distinguish between literal fact and personal opinion when asking and answering questions. To be able to answer evaluation questions using personal experiences and reference to the text.

WHAT YOU NEED
Photocopiable page 53; individual whiteboards; writing materials.

Whenever the author of a newspaper article writes about the feelings, thoughts, behaviours and motives of any individuals, groups or organisations it is possible to have evaluation.

DON'T PANIC!
■ Revisit the lesson 'Literal and inferential intention in non-fiction' on page 40. Revisit the lessons on evaluation on pages 42–49.

INTRODUCTION
In this lesson, the children analyse an extract from a newspaper report on the highly emotive subject of genetic modification, to examine how evaluation can be used in non-fiction writing to persuade and influence the reader's opinion.

WHAT TO DO
■ It would be helpful for the children to have completed the activities in the lesson 'Literal and inferential intention in non-fiction' (page 40) before starting this lesson.
■ Explain the difference between a fact and an opinion. You may wish to use an example such as 'Thierry Henry is a football player' as a fact and 'Arsenal is the best football team in the world' as an opinion.
■ Give each child a whiteboard. Say the name of a topic or subject of interest and ask the children to write either a fact or an opinion about it. Ask them to hold up their boards and check that they understand what a fact and what an opinion are.
■ Remind the children that during their SATs comprehension paper, it is very likely that they will be given a non-fiction text of some kind. Tell them they are going to analyse a newspaper article. Remind them that authors of non-fiction use both literal and inference in their writing. Ask the children if they think it is possible for them to include evaluation too, and if so, how would it be presented?
■ Explain that whenever the author of a newspaper article writes about peoples' feelings, thoughts, behaviours or motives, it is possible to have evaluation. It is useful to note that the feelings and thoughts of the people are usually presented by the opinions expressed in the article and their behaviour is shown through the factual statements.
■ Ask the children to work in pairs, and give each pair a copy of photocopiable page 53. Ask them to use two different-coloured pens to highlight the information they think is factual and the information they consider to be personal opinion.
■ After ten minutes, discuss the following points as a class. How much of the article is fact and how much is opinion? Can the children summarise the opinions of the people involved? Explain that journalists are meant to provide an impartial view of the events but that on many occasions their articles can be rather emotive and echo the opinions of their readers. Ask the children to explain what they think the view of the journalist is. How do they know that?
■ Ask the children to return to their pairs and use the highlighted information to practise asking and answering evaluation questions. Remind the children that when they answer they should refer to their own opinions and experiences that the author might agree with. Questions might include: 'Why do you think the animal lovers are concerned about genetic modification of cats and dogs?' or 'Why do you think health officials welcomed the development?'

PLENARY
■ Ask the children to evaluate what they have read. What is their opinion on genetic modification and selective breeding? Can they explain why they feel this way by drawing upon their own experiences and by referring to the text?

Designer Kitties – Not To Be Sniffed At

DESIGNER label fanatics and cute kitty lovers with more money than sense can now add the world's first designer cat to their self-indulgent collection. Following the strange-looking 'hairless' cat that was the product of selective breeding, a canny American company have achieved the impossible and turned household moggies into anti-sneeze super-kitties designed for cat-owners who suffer from sniffles, tears and asthma attacks.

The company making a £7,500 per cat mint from the enterprise said, "For the first time, people who have allergies will be able to keep a cat without suffering. This is a scientific breakthrough for which we should win an award."

Health officials have welcomed this recent development despite the cost, following research published last month showing that babies could be at 50% greater risk of developing skin allergies if their family has a cat.

However animal lovers on both sides of the Atlantic are concerned that if the 'designer pet' craze continues with

scientists playing around with genetic modification and selective breeding, health effects on cats, dogs and other animals involved in this money-spinning racket could be seriously affected as interbreeding continues.

The Daily Newsround, June 5, 2006

PREDICTION – THE BIGGER PICTURE

OBJECTIVES
To be able to link visual clues, key words in the title and genre to make predictions.

WHAT YOU NEED
Photocopiable page 55; a selection of fiction and non-fiction books with intriguing titles; individual whiteboards; writing materials.

By using all sorts of clues that can be found from the title, cover, contents page, illustrations, photographs and diagrams of a book, magazine or newspaper, you can get an idea of what to expect from the text inside.

DON'T PANIC!
■ If the children find it difficult to use the key words in the title to make predictions, go back to the lesson 'Key words paint the picture' on page 8.

INTRODUCTION
Why is it important to be able to make predictions? When the children are presented with the SATs comprehension paper they will instantly begin to make astute predictions about the contents of the text and the sorts of questions they will be asked and so be better equipped to recognise unfamiliar vocabulary that goes with the subject of the text.

WHAT TO DO
■ Tell the children that part of being a good Text Detective is being able to think ahead. By using all sorts of clues that can be found firstly from the title, cover and contents page, as well as illustrations, photographs and diagrams inside a book, magazine or newspaper, a reader can begin to have an idea of what to expect from the text inside.

■ Select a small number of books – they could be fiction or non-fiction. Choose one book at a time and without letting the children see the book, read the title. Ask the children to work with a friend, and give them one minute to work out and write down what they think the book is about.

■ Ask the children to share their predictions and explain which clues they used from the title. For example, can they tell if the book is fiction or non-fiction? Do they use the key words from the title and what pictures do they create in their heads as they hear them? Is it possible to tell the genre of the book by just the title?

■ Now show the children the cover of the book. Give the pairs two minutes to use the clues on the cover to change or add to their prediction. How did the cover help them to refine or correct their prediction? Discuss the features they might have looked at: the words of any subtitle, the main image, font size and style, use of photography or illustrations, imagery and symbols.

■ Finally, read the blurb and see how close the children were to the additional information given here.

■ Repeat the exercise with several other books.

■ Hand out photocopiable page 55 to each pair and ask them to fill in the boxes with annotations to explain the features of the book cover that the arrows point to. They should repeat the same process of analysis that they have been using in the shared examples.

PLENARY
■ Discuss the children's findings. Do they all agree? Talk through the annotated cover, discussing the main points that have been picked out.

■ First of all it is noticeable that this is a fiction book because unlike information books, the picture is not explained by the title.

■ The soft-focus photograph of a young girl, set against ruins, implies that the book contains historical facts mixed with fiction. The genre, therefore, may be a fictional historical adventure (possibly set in World War II).

■ The title could refer to the girl's eventual freedom, or maybe it refers to war planes, or perhaps it is simply making the link with her growing up and finding independence during a time of hardship.

Wings to Fly

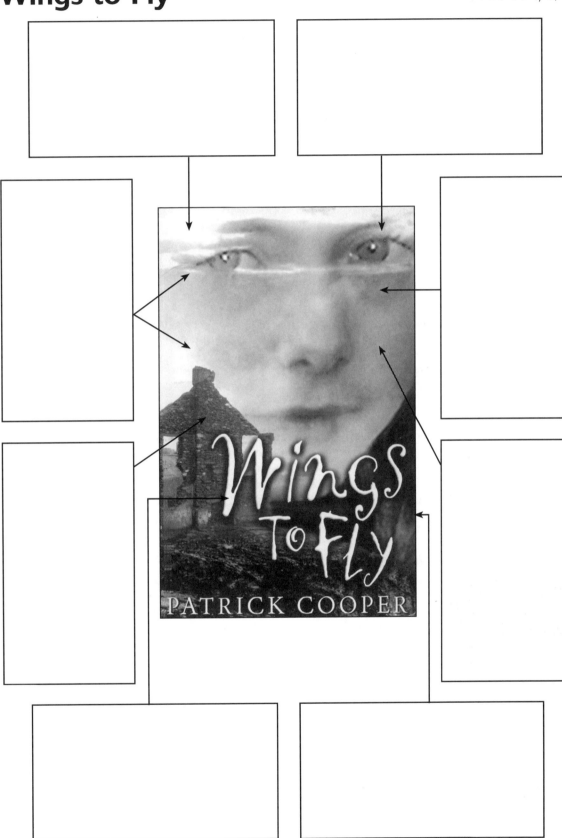

Image © 2001, Andersen Press

READING BETWEEN THE LINES

The children should be able to apply their powers of prediction (as practised in the context of making judgements based on book covers) to passages of text, picking up on key-word clues to predict quite specific events. This skill will help them to take a more active approach to reading texts, which is invaluable in the SATs comprehension paper.

OBJECTIVES
To be able to make predictions by linking setting, characters, feelings and actions within a text.

WHAT YOU NEED
Photocopiable pages 57–59; writing materials.

WHAT TO DO
■ Remind the children of the book *Wings to Fly* as used in the lesson 'Prediction – the bigger picture' on page 54.
■ Explain that, as we know, authors like to use inference to make their writing more interesting for the reader. Instead of putting everything 'right there' in the text, they like to leave subtle clues for the reader to interpret.
■ Tell the children that authors often use inference to suggest or imply what might happen next. They want the reader to make links between the setting, characters, feelings and actions to work out what will happen next in the plot.
■ In the short term this helps to build suspense and tension at dramatic moments in the text. Here, authors use exciting, descriptive language with key-word references to suggest what might happen immediately afterwards.
■ In the long term, the use of 'inferential prediction' allows authors to build up the plot as a whole – it helps the reader to link each event with another. In this way the reader feels more personally involved in the development of the story.
■ Hand out photocopiable page 57. Ask the children to read through the first extract from *Wings to Fly*, looking out for clues in the text as to what might happen next. They should highlight these clues, and use them to predict what might happen to John. Remind them to back up their predictions with evidence from the text.
■ Next, hand out photocopiable page 58. Explain to the children that this second extract from *Wings to Fly* is about what actually happened to John. Ask the children to read this passage and highlight the key words that tell them what happened to John, thinking about how these key words link to the clues in the first extract.

PLENARY
■ Discuss the children's findings for both the extracts. Can they see clear links between what actually happened to John in the second extract, and what might have happened to him, as suggested by the first extract? They should be able to see that clues from the first extract were picked up on and resolved in the second.
■ If necessary, model the process of finding clues and linking them to what actually happened on enlarged copies of the extracts.

When answering literal questions, the key words appear in the text, question and answer.

DON'T PANIC!
■ If the children find it difficult to use the first extract to make predictions as to what might happen next, use photocopiable page 59 for a differentiated version of the activity.

Wings to Fly extract 1

John was at the nests now. The gulls were shrieking and diving at him, but he took no notice, just stretched for the nearest nest, took an egg and slid it carefully into his pocket.

He took off his cap and waved down to me, grinning happily.

He reached for another. This one was above him. The mother gull was flapping in his face as he twisted and pulled himself up.

He was at the top of the hard granite, reaching the shale above it. He was so excited with getting the eggs, that he forgot to test the rock, and didn't realise it was loose.

He stretched out to wave at me again.

'Watch out!' I yelled.

He didn't hear. He couldn't have heard anything over the screaming of the seagulls and the roar of the sea.

■ Write what you think might happen next to John. Use clues from the text to back up your predictions.

Wings to Fly extract 2

'What happened?' he muttered.

'You fell, John. You fell off the blooming cliff.' He lifted an arm, watching it to make sure it was doing what it was supposed to do. He reached into his coat pocket, and pulled out a sticky mess of yolk and eggshell.

'I bust the egg, Sarah,' he said, trying to smile. 'I'd better go up and get another one.' Then he tried to stand up. He got as far as his knees, then he fell backwards, groaning.

'Are you all right, John?' I asked stupidly. I was looking at his leg. There was something wrong about it…

'What are we going to do, John? You'll never get back across the rocks.'

'I'll be all right in a minute,' he said.

'You won't,' I said. 'You've broken your leg. You'll never walk like that. I'd best go and get help.'

Text © Patrick Cooper

■ Write how what actually happened to John links back to the clues from the first passage.

Find the clues

■ Read the following sentences from *Wings to Fly*.

■ Highlight the key word clues in each sentence that build the tension. From your own knowledge and experience, write down what you think might happen next.

■ Back up your answers with evidence from the text. The first answer has been completed as an example.

1. John was at the nests now. **The gulls were shrieking and diving at him**, but he took **no notice**, just stretched for the nearest nest, took an **egg** and **slid it carefully into his pocket.**

I think that the shrieking and diving of the gulls is a warning to John not to go any further, which suggests that because John is ignoring this, he will get into trouble. I think the mention of how carefully he slips the egg into his pocket suggests that it will break in the end.

2. He took off his cap and waved down to me, grinning happily.

I think that...

3. He reached for another. This one was above him. The mother gull was flapping in his face as he twisted and pulled himself up.

   He was at the top of the hard granite, reaching the shale above it. He was so excited with getting the eggs, that he forgot to test the rock, and didn't realise it was loose.

I think that...

4. He stretched out to wave at me again.

I think that...

5. 'Watch out!' I yelled.
   He didn't hear. He couldn't have heard anything over the screaming of the seagulls and the roar of the sea.

I think that...

■ On a separate sheet of paper, write what you think might happen next.

MAKING SENSE OF WORDS AND PHRASES IN FICTION

The children are likely to encounter unfamiliar vocabulary in their SATs comprehension paper, and it is important that this does not cause them to panic. This lesson teaches them techniques for making sense of unfamiliar words and phrases. Once they see that they can easily deduce the meaning of words they don't know, they will be less intimidated in an exam situation.

OBJECTIVES
To be able to make sense of unfamiliar words and phrases in fiction, using contextual clues.

WHAT YOU NEED
Photocopiable pages 61 and 65; writing materials.

WHAT TO DO
■ Explain to the children that when they sit their SATs comprehension paper it will be quite normal for them to come across words, phrases or descriptions that they find hard to understand. Emphasise that if this happens they should not panic. They should stay calm and try to work out from the clues in the text what the words and phrases could mean. Reassure the children by telling them that during this lesson you will show them tricks to help them find the meaning of difficult words and phrases.

■ Display an enlarged copy of the extract on photocopiable page 61. Explain to the children that you are going to use it to show them how to find the meaning of an unfamiliar word.

■ Read the extract together. Do not explain or discuss any of the complicated vocabulary as you might usually do when sharing a text.

■ Now highlight the first sentence: 'A lion was sleeping in his lair when a mouse mistakenly ran over the mighty beast's nose and awakened him.' Underline the word 'lair', and explain to the class that you are not sure what the word 'lair' means, but that you are going to try to work it out.

■ First, explain that you are going to go back to the beginning of the sentence and read it again. In this way you might gather more information that will help you guess what the word means. For example: 'A lion was sleeping in his lair' which suggests that it is a place or object; it was 'his lair' – therefore it belongs to the lion.

■ Next, read the sentence again but leave the word out, replacing it with the first letter sound or blend. For example: 'The lion was sleeping in his l- when a mouse...'

■ To find out what the word means, explain that you can replace it with another word that makes sense and that fits in with the meaning of the sentence. Demonstrate this with some words that might work ('cave', 'home', 'bed'). Explain that you can check for sense by seeing if the new word looks right, and if it sounds right. These replacement words are similar to the original word and should help you work out what it means.

■ Hand out copies of photocopiable page 61 to pairs of children. Ask them to work together to read the story again. They should use the strategies you have just shown them to find alternative words to replace words from the text and to define the meaning of phrases, using information in the text.

PLENARY
■ Ask each pair to join with another and discuss their findings in these small groups. Encourage them to check the correct definitions of the words in a dictionary.

Don't panic when you come across words and phrases you don't understand. Use the strategies you have learned to work out what they mean.

DON'T PANIC!
■ As a reminder of the techniques to find the meaning of unknown vocabulary, use photocopiable page 65. Give children their own copy or make an enlarged version and display it.

The lion and the Mouse

A lion was sleeping in his <u>lair</u> when a mouse mistakenly ran over the mighty beast's nose and awakened him. the lion grabbed the frightened little creature with his paw and was just about to crush him when the mouse began pleading for mercy and <u>declared</u> the <u>he had not consciously intended</u> to <u>offend</u> the lion. Moreover, the mouse <u>sought</u> to <u>convince</u> the lion not to stain his <u>honourable</u> paws with such an <u>insignificant</u> prey. Smiling at his little prisoner's fright, the lion generously let him go.

Now, a short time after this <u>occurrence</u> the lion was caught in a net laid by some hunters while roaming the woods in search of prey. Finding himself entangled in rope without the hope of escape, the lion let out a roar that <u>resounded</u> throughout the entire forest. Recognizing the voice of his former <u>saviour</u>, the mouse ran to the spot, and <u>without much ado</u>, began nibbling the knots that had <u>ensnared</u> the lion. In a short time he freed the noble beast and thus convinced him that kindness is seldom wasted and that, no matter how <u>meagre</u> a creature may be, he may have it in his power to <u>return a good deed</u>.

Little friends may prove great friends.

Aesop

1. Read the extract above and carefully read again the sentences that contain the underlined words. Write another word that has the same meaning next to each word below.

declared _____   honourable _____   saviour _____

offend _____   insignificant _____   ensnared _____

sought _____   occurrence _____   meagre _____

convince _____   resounded _____

2. Explain the following phrases.
... he had not consciously intended...

_____

... without much ado...

_____

... return a good deed...

_____

MAKING SENSE OF WORDS AND PHRASES IN NON-FICTION

The children are likely to encounter unfamiliar vocabulary in their SATs comprehension paper, and it is important that this does not cause them to panic. They should be equally confident dealing with new words and phrases in technical non-fiction texts as they are in fiction texts. This lesson builds on the techniques they have already learned to make sense of unfamiliar words and phrases in a wider variety of texts.

OBJECTIVES
To make sense of unfamiliar words and phrases in non-fiction using contextual clues.

WHAT YOU NEED
Photocopiable pages 63–65; writing materials.

WHAT TO DO

■ It would be helpful for the children to have completed the activities in the lesson 'Making sense of words and phrases in fiction' on page 60 before completing the activities in this lesson.

■ Explain to the children that during this lesson they will learn how to solve the meanings of unknown words and phrases in non-fiction texts. Tell them that with non-fiction it is much easier to predict what the content of the text will be than with fiction, because the authors usually write fact-based text that is directly related to the title. This knowledge should make it easier for them to start thinking about the information, words and phrases they might be faced with before they even begin to read the text.

■ Tell the children that they are going to work with a newspaper article with the headline 'Day the moon took a bite out of the sun'. Write this line on the board and ask the children to describe the image that forms in their head when they hear the title. Can they predict what the rest of the text will be about? (A report of a partial solar eclipse.)

■ Divide the class into teams of four. Each team should have a scribe. Hand out photocopiable page 64 to each team and ask the children to recall everything they already know about eclipses and all of the technical vocabulary they may expect to come across in the text. The scribe should record their findings on the sheet. Allow ten minutes for this activity.

■ Now hand out photocopiable page 63 to each group. One child from each group should read the text to the others. Remind them to take account of the grammar, speech marks, exclamation marks, commas and so on, as this will help them to make more sense of the text from the start. Ask them to use what they already know from the information in the text and their prediction skills to have a go at defining the meaning of the underlined words and phrases in the extract. The scribe should record these when the group has agreed on answers.

■ Now the teams can fill in the second table on photocopiable page 64, recording what new words, phrases and facts they have found out from the article.

PLENARY

■ As a class, discuss the children's findings and any new words or phrases.

■ Encourage the children to check the meanings of new words in a dictionary. Discuss the strategies used to understand the meanings of any new words and phrases.

Don't panic when you come across words and phrases you don't understand. Use the strategies you have practised to work out what they mean.

DON'T PANIC!
■ As a reminder of the techniques to use to find the meaning of unknown vocabulary, use photocopiable page 65. Give children their own copy or make an enlarged version and display it.

Daily Mail, Thursday March 30, 2006

Day the moon took a bite out of the sun

SKYWATCHERS were treated to a partial solar eclipse yesterday. The moon blocked out around 17 per cent of the sun in a phenomenon best seen in the south of England.

A much more spectacular total eclipse, however, was seen in a narrow zone stretching north-east from Brazil to Mongolia via Turkey.

It lasted for more than four minutes in the southern Libyan desert – the best global viewing point. The moon took more than 90 minutes to pass over the face of the sun.

Dr. Robert Massey, of Greenwich Royal Observatory, said solar eclipses were 'the ultimate astronomical show'. Speaking from Turkey, where the total eclipse lasted three minutes and 45 seconds, he said: 'Despite knowing exactly how eclipses happen, scientists are fascinated by them.

'They provide the best chance to view the innermost part of the sun's corona, which is much hotter than the sun's surface.

'Even though it's only for three or four minutes, an eclipse provides us with the best opportunity to get in there and have a look around.'

Concerns were raised yesterday that warnings against watching eclipses with the naked eye were not strong enough.

Chief Medical Officer Sir Liam Donaldson said new official guidance would be issued in future.

The next partial eclipse is in August 2008.

Ben Quinn

■ Explain what you think the following words or phrases mean in the context of the report.

partial solar eclipse _____

narrow zone _____

global _____

Greenwich Royal Observatory _____

'the ultimate astronomical show' _____

sun's corona _____

naked eye _____

official _____

Name _____

What we know and what we have found out

What we **know** about:		
Facts	Vocabulary	Meanings

What we **have found out** about:		
New facts	New vocabulary	New meanings

How to solve unknown words

If you get stuck reading a word, you can:

■ Go back to the beginning of the sentence. Read it again – to gather more information.

■ Leave the word out and read on to the end of the sentence.

■ If you know the first letter sound or blend say that – and then read on to the end of the sentence.

Next, ask yourself:

■ What other word would make sense in its place?
   Does it fit in with the meaning of the sentence?

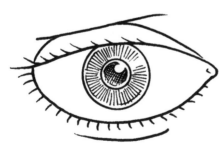

■ Does the new word look right? Is it speltled that way?

■ Does the new word sound right? Can we say it that way?
   Put it in the sentence – is the grammar correct?

PLANS

SUMMARISING THE TEXT

During this lesson the children will learn how to identify the key facts and information in a text and use this to give an accurate and brief recount of the passage they have read. They will subsequently know exactly where to find the answers to questions when it really matters. In addition to this, they will be equipped to take notes and know how to use a text for research purposes.

WHAT TO DO

■ Explain to the children that they are going to learn how to summarise a piece of text, and that this skill will help them to locate the important information in a piece of text in order to answer questions quickly and accurately.

■ Tell them that to be able to give a brief and accurate summary of the main idea within a passage, they need to be able to find the key information and facts. Explain that this simply means identifying the answers to the following questions and ignoring the unnecessary details. Write these questions on the board: 'Who is involved?' 'What is happening?' 'Where is it happening?' 'Why is it happening?' 'When is it happening?'

■ Hand out photocopiable pages 67 and 69 to pairs of children. Read the text aloud as a whole class, then ask the children to read it again to themselves. Afterwards, be sure to clarify any unknown words or difficult phrases.

■ Draw the children's attention to the title of the article. Explain that a title often gives useful information that helps you to make a summary, and that often as readers we forget to use it!

■ Tell the children that the rest of the article will discuss whether or not television is the only friend of OAPs and it is now their job to identify the important who, what, why, when and where information and discard the additional details. Ask the pairs to work together to cross out the unnecessary details with a black pen.

■ After this, ask the children to use a coloured pen to highlight the words and phrases they are left after the unnecessary details have been deleted. Explain that with lots of practise, they will be able simply to highlight the important information without having to cross out the unnecessary details first.

■ Finally ask the children to check that they have only the most important summarising information left by sorting and writing them into the 'who', 'what', 'why', 'when' and 'where' columns on photocopiable page 69.

PLENARY

■ Ask the children to use the information in the boxes on photocopiable page 69 to summarise the article.

■ Ask one child from each pair to give a brief, accurate recount of the article to the other. Their partner should then ask some questions about the text and they should be able to find the answers very quickly.

■ Finally, discuss the findings as a class. Were all the pairs left with the same information?

OBJECTIVES
To be able to highlight key elements of a text in order to give a succinct and accurate recount of a passage.

WHAT YOU NEED
Photocopiable pages 67–69; black writing materials.

POINTS
If you are asked to give a summary of a text, it means to give a brief and accurate recount of the main points. Identify the important who, what, why, when and where information and discard the unnecessary details.

DON'T PANIC!
■ If the children find it difficult to summarise this text, use photocopiable page 68 for a less challenging extract. This could also be used in conjunction with photocopiable page 69 as further practise of the technique covered in the lesson.

Daily Mail, Thursday March 30, 2006

TV, the only friend for millions of OAPs

ALMOST half of pensioners rely on the television as their only source of company, according to research published yesterday.

The disturbing figures reveal the true extent of the loneliness faced by Britain's ten million elderly on a daily basis.

The survey suggests that 500,000 pensioners who live on their own see their family only once a month, and more than a million feel trapped.

Of those, 227,000 no longer feel comfortable leaving their front door due to poor health (45 per cent), a lack of money (eight per cent) or no help (eight per cent). 'Obviously the picture varies from family to family,' said Paul Cann, director of policy at Help the Aged, which commissioned the survey.

'But a significant number of elderly people are being left horrifically isolated – whether it be because of family breakdown, society's attitudes to them or geographical displacement.

'Whichever way you look at it, these figures are truly shocking and there is absolutely no excuse for it. It's a damning indictment of our society that we can leave people to feel like this.'

The survey asked a random sample of people aged 65 and over for details of their normal weekly routine and attitudes to the changing role of the family.

Almost ten per cent said they saw their grandchildren less than every six months and were not happy asking them to visit more in fear of pestering them.

Distance was also a key factor driving the generations apart, as 30 per cent said that their grandchildren lived too far away to make it easy to visit.

The survey, carried out in January, was published by Help the Aged to mark April's 'Helping Unite Generations' campaign.

Paul Sims

Name _____

The wind and the sun

The wind and the sun once had an argument as to which was the stronger of the two, and they agreed to settle the issue by holding a contest: whoever could make a traveller take off his coat first would be recognised as the most powerful. The wind began and blew with all his might until he stirred up a blast, cold and fierce as an Alaskan storm. The stronger he blew, however, the tighter the traveller wrapped his coat around him and clasped it with his hands. Then the sun broke out, and with his welcome beams he dispersed the clouds and the cold. The traveller felt the sudden warmth, and as the sun shone brighter and brighter, he sat down, overcome by the heat, and threw his coat on the ground.

Thus the sun was declared the winner, and ever since then, persuasion has been held in higher esteem than force. Indeed, sunshine of a kind and gentle manner will sooner open a man's heart than all the threats and force of blustering authority.

Aesop

Who? What? Why? When? Where?

■ Use a coloured pen to highlight the important information in the text. Then arrange the information into the appropriate columns below.

■ Use these facts to write a summary of the text.

Who (is involved)?	**What** (is happening)?	**Why** (is this happening)?	**When** (is this happening)?	**Where** (is this happening)?

■ SCHOLASTIC
www.scholastic.co.uk

QUICK FIX FOR YEAR 6: COMPREHENSION

USING THE RECIPROCAL READING FRAMEWORK

The Reciprocal Reading Process is a method that enables the children to consolidate everything they have learned about exploring a piece of text fully. They are guided through the process of analysing a piece of text – from searching for key words, to clarifying and summarising – in order to devise literal, inference and evaluation questions on the text. They then swap questions with other children, answer them, and finally mark them, assessing each other's and their own performance critically, in order to identify areas of strength and weakness.

WHAT TO DO
■ Arrange the children into mixed-ability teams of four. Tell the teams that they will be working together, using all of the skills and knowledge they have learned about reading comprehension.
■ Explain that they will use a method to explore a text together by making predictions, clarifying and summarising. They will then use the text to write literal, inference and evaluation questions for another team to answer. Explain that the teams will be competing against each other for points.
■ Ask the teams to work together to compile a set of class rules that the children should adhere to when using the Reciprocal Reading Process. For example, how will points for answers be awarded? Suggest that the answers should be written in full sentences, using key words from the question, evidence from the text with correct spelling and punctuation to gain full marks.
■ Hand out photocopiable pages 71 and 72 to each team, plus a book from your selection. Ask the children to record their team name at the top of photocopiable page 71, the name of the book and the page number they are working from.
■ Now ask the children to work as a team through the prompts on the photocopiable sheet. They should clarify any difficult words or phrases, summarise and predict what might happen next. Remind them to support their answers using evidence from the text. They can use more paper if they need to.
■ Next, ask the teams to use photocopiable page 72 to write an inference, literal and evaluative question about their passage of text. They should also write the answers to these questions on a separate piece of paper.
■ Ask the teams to swap their books and questions and allow them ten minutes to write their answers, according to the class rules.
■ Finally, ask them to swap back and mark the work. The number of points should be calculated and written on the work with an explanation. For example: 'A good answer to the literal question. We only took away 2 marks; you spelled a word wrongly when it was in the text and you forgot to put a full stop at the end of the sentence.'

PLENARY
■ Discuss a selection of questions and answers from each group and work through any excellent examples or problems that may have arisen.
■ This method can be used in future on any texts; encourage the children to select their own for further practise.

Text detectives

Team name _____

Title of book _____

Description of cover _____

What genre (type) of text is it? _____

Prediction – what's the text about? _____

Choose a page from the book for the following tasks. _____

Clarifying

Choose words or phrases you don't understand and work out what they mean. Write your definitions in the table below.

Word/phrase	What I think it means

Summarising

Write down the main ideas in the passage.

_____

_____

_____

_____

Predicting

What might happen next? (Base this on your own experience and clues in the text.)

_____

_____

_____

_____

SCHOLASTIC
www.scholastic.co.uk

Name _____

Exploring the text

Think of literal, inference and evaluation questions to ask about your text.

Literal (Who? What? Where? 'Right there'!)

Q. _____

_____

_____

A. _____

_____

_____

Inference (Think and search for clues)

Q. _____

_____

_____

A. _____

_____

_____

Evaluation (On your own – from your own experience, with evidence from the text)

Q. _____

_____

_____

A. _____

_____

_____

Text genres

The following are examples of different kinds of text:

narrative text

humorous	fantasy
mystery	horror
science fiction	classic
myth/legend	adventure
historic	fable
poetry	play
fairy/folk tale	biography
autobiography	

information text

recount	report
instructions	explanation
argument	discussion

Each narrative genre has its own particular characteristics and functions that are reflected in the way the author makes use of language to link and develop themes, characters/personalities, plot, mood and settings to engage the reader.

Here are examples of the characteristics of some of the narrative genres.

Adventure stories

Language features: twisting, turning plot; constant excitement and danger; a series of complicated, difficult events and problems; full of suspense; story-clues are often indicated through characters' dialogue.

■ The purpose of an adventure/thriller story is to entertain the audience through action and suspense that revolve around a series of carefully connected clues.

■ Little time is spent on description, unless it supports the building of tension that accompanies each adventure.

■ The plot unfolds quickly and dramatically, generally leading to the hero/heroine reaching safety and 'saving the day' for others.

Plays

Language features: meaning through setting; action and dialogue; stage directions.

■ A play is a script used generally for storytelling through dialogue and dramatic performance.

■ Often adapted from a novel or short story, the play is delivered to the audience through the use of sets, sound, lighting effects and costumes.

■ Limited by the dimensions of time and space, plays are not able to include every scene from a novel, and need to rely on fewer sub-plots and more carefully chosen, meaningful scenes to carry the story.

■ At such times a dramatic performance can sometimes enhance the written word and make an even greater impact on the audience because of it.

Historical fiction

Language features: detailed reference to time and place; plot details embedded in history (for example, escape from oppression, victory in war, characters improving status socially, scientific breakthrough).

■ Historical fiction is generally written to entertain and inform by authors of the present day.

■ References to real personalities and events in history are made within the plot, with the characters (often fictitious) providing us with a real insight of the extent of the problems and struggles of the time.

Science fiction

Language features: technical/technological-based vocabulary including invented words (for example, electronic sub-etha device, starship, intergalactic); ideas beyond present-day scientific reality; detailed description of abstract concepts and events.

■ Narrative is written to entertain and in some cases to inform – based on exploration of scientific or futuristic possibilities – with story plots revolving around dimensions beyond our everyday world.

■ A common theme involves the force of good to overcome evil, where the hero/heroine makes use of their advanced scientific

knowledge and often great physical agility in a series of spectacular battles to protect our world or other planets in the galaxy from total destruction.

Classics *(includes poetry and plays, for example Shakespeare)*

Language features: largely traditional/formal/poetic writing style reflecting the spoken language of the time in history when it was written; detailed lively descriptions of characters and settings; covers wide range of cultural beliefs, morals and way of life.

■ The purpose of classic books is to entertain and sometimes to remind the reader of true morals and values.

■ The range of narrative covers adventure, fantasy, mystery and legend.

■ Charles Dickens is a good example of how classic authors liked to use a combination of humour to entertain, against a backdrop of the often grim reality of the times. His story themes generally reflect the cruelty and selfishness of the society of his age and the desperate poverty and hardship that was ignored in pursuit of wealth and status.

■ The frequent message from classic authors is that good eventually wins over fear, bullying and temptation.

Fantasy

Language features: adventurous, exciting escape from reality to other worlds where time in the real world often stands still; detailed description of magical characters and settings; involvement of supernatural forces (for example, ghosts, witches and sorcery) and creatures that can talk and transform.

■ Fantasy provides escape and entertainment for the reader into other worlds and extraordinary landscapes where anything is possible.

■ Sometimes involves a journey of discovery for children of 'the real world' who encounter magical experiences in a series of unbelievable events and dangerous challenges that test their courage and values – and help them to resolve personal problems back in their own world on their return.

Humorous *(stories, poetry, plays)*

Language features: full of funny sub-plots and surprises; exaggeration of reality to emphasise the good and the bad in people (for example, vivid and sometimes grotesque descriptions of the bad characters); range of colourful, expressive vocabulary; frequent play on words and use of metaphors and similes to describe settings, characters, their actions and behaviour in an extreme way, or to understate, suggesting that the ridiculous and seemingly unlikely may in some way be close enough to reality to be possible.

■ The purpose of humorous writing is to entertain and amuse, calling on the reader's personal experience of life to grasp the joke within a series of fast-moving, well-paced incidents and unusual events that they can relate to or imagine happening.

■ The dialogue is often informal and jaunty and sometimes ridiculous, often sprinkled with implied clues to set up the punchline that is coming.

■ Since they usually concentrate on a plot that highlights human relationships and people's reactions to each other's behaviour, humorous stories often contain wisdom and reveal an element of truth about life.

Fables

Language features: originally passed on by word of mouth, rather than written, fables have little descriptive detail; sentence length is short and although the sentence structure is quite simple, the language tends to be formal.

■ A fable is a short story that aims to both entertain and to enlighten and advise the reader.

■ About three thousand years ago a Greek slave called Aesop became well known for his animal fables that he told about the wisdom and foolishness of people.

■ The purpose of a fable is to deliver a simple message within a moral or piece of advice at the end of the story.

INTRODUCING THE PRACTICE PAPERS

This lesson can be used to introduce any of the example SATs comprehension papers in the section that follows. If you keep to a similar format each time you work on a paper, the children will become familiar with the style of the paper and being in an exam situation. You should also remind them each time of good exam techniques.

WHAT TO DO
■ Tell the children that during the lesson they will be given the opportunity to practise all of the comprehension skills and knowledge they have learntedby completing a SATs comprehension paper. They have been designed to support the children's revision by supplying them with a range of question types across a variety of text genre. Reassure the children and talk them through these excellent techniques for sitting exams.

■ Tell the children that these are good, tried and tested exam techniques.

■ Read the text and the questions twice before you start to answer them – sometimes one question may answer another!

■ As you read the text, make notes of the key people involved, what is happening, where it is happening, when and why, with a pencil at the side of the page.

■ As you read, try to predict the literal, inference and evaluative questions you could be asked and remember where you saw the answers.

■ Pick out the key words in the question and skim and scan the text for the same words, or those that have a similar meaning.

■ Write your answers in full sentences – it will really help you to keep on track. Check that key words from the question are in your answer.

■ Look at the number of marks allocated for each question – should your answer combine facts from more than one place in the text?

■ Try to work out if the question is literal, inference or evaluation. Should the answer be 'right there'? Will you have to think and search for clues and will you need to use your own personal experiences that the author would agree with?

■ Use evidence from the text to explain how you know the answer is correct. Quotes provide direct, concise evidence and prevent waffle!

■ Write neatly – the person marking your SATs comprehension paper may have 300 papers to look at!

■ Use spellings from the paper.

■ Next, hand out the practice paper and ask the children to use the text to answer the questions. At this stage, how you use the papers is up to you. You could use exam conditions and set an appropriate time or you could let the children work through the questions informally, in pairs or teams.

PLENARY
Choose from the following activities.

■ Work through questions and answers from the paper as a whole class, or with individuals/groups.

■ Allow the children to mark each other's work.

■ Look for and use similar questions from past SATs comprehension papers.

■ Ask the children to use the text to write additional questions and answers of their own.

Practice paper 1

■ Read the following extract about Kasper Whiskey whose quiet life living with his mother Pumpkin changes for ever when he is enticed into The City and the dangerous world of King Streetwise.

■ Remember to skim and scan for context clues to clarify unknown words; to predict what will happen next and to predict possible literal, inference and evaluation questions that you may be asked.

Kasper in the Glitter

by Philip Ridley

Chapter 19, page 88

'Don't move!' warned Jingo.

Kasper didn't need telling. He was too scared to move even if he wanted to.

'Gracious me!' muttered Jingo, standing very still. 'I've told Knucklehead a million times not to let the dogs in the kitchen.'

'Are they… dangerous?' asked Kasper, barely moving his lips.

'Not if you keep very, very still. The last time this happened I had to stay still for nearly three hours.'

'Three hours!' exclaimed Kasper. (Or as near exclamation as he could get without moving his lips.)

Sweat started to trickle down Kasper's face.

And arms.

He felt his shirt sticking to him.

His hands became moist.

And that's when the basket started to slip through his fingers…

Text © Philip Ridley Image © Chris Riddell

■ SCHOLASTIC
www.scholastic.co.uk

Practice paper 1

■ Re-read the passage and then read the questions below carefully.

■ To guide your answer, remember to highlight the key word clues in the questions, then skim and scan the text to find the same or similar clues for your answers.

■ Think about the type of question you are answering. Is it a literal question or an inference or evaluation question asking you for evidence to support your answer?

■ These questions are about the extract from *Kasper in the Glitter* by Philip Ridley. Answer the questions and note down what type of question you think each one is.

Write your answers on a separate sheet of paper.

1. Who warned Kasper not to move?   *(1 mark)*

2. Do you think that Jingo's friend Knucklehead was careless? Why do you say that?   *(2 marks)*

3. Why do you think that Kasper didn't want to move around in the kitchen? How do you know that?   *(2 marks)*

4. Do you think that the dogs are dangerous? Why?

                                      (2 marks)

5. Do you think that Kasper had visited Jingo and Knucklehead before? How do you know?   *(2 marks)*

6. Give three reasons why you think the dogs are aggressive.   *(3 marks)*

TOTAL

www.scholastic.co.uk

QUICK FIX FOR YEAR 6: COMPREHENSION

Name _____

Practice paper 2

■ Read the following extract, remembering to skim and scan for context clues to clarify unknown words; to predict what will happen next and to predict possible literal, inference and evaluation questions that you might be asked.

The Hobbit

by JRR Tolkien

CHAPTER 1
AN UNEXPECTED PARTY

In a hole in the ground there lived a hobbit. Not a nasty, dirty, wet hole, filled with the ends of worms and an oozy smell, nor yet a dry, bare, sandy hole with nothing in it to sit down on or to eat: it was a hobbit-hole, and that means comfort.

It had a perfectly round door like a porthole, painted green, with a shiny yellow brass knob in the exact middle. The door opened on to a tube-shaped hall like a tunnel: a very comfortable tunnel without smoke, with panelled walls, and floors tiled and carpeted, provided with polished chairs, and lots and lots of pegs for hats and coats – the hobbit was fond of visitors. The tunnel wound on and on, going fairly but not quite straight into the side of the hill – The Hill, as all the people for many miles round called it – and many little round doors opened out of it, first on one side and then on another. No going upstairs for the hobbit: bedrooms, bathrooms, cellars, pantries (lots of these), wardrobes (he had whole rooms devoted to clothes), kitchens, dining-rooms, all were on the same floor, and indeed on the same passage. The best rooms were all on the left-hand side (going in), for these were the only ones to have windows, deep-set round windows looking over his garden, and meadows beyond, sloping down to the river.

This hobbit was a very well-to-do hobbit, and his name was Baggins. The Bagginses had lived in the neighbourhood of The Hill for time out of mind, and people considered them very respectable, not only because most of them were rich, but also because they never had any adventures or did anything unexpected: you could tell what a Baggins would say on any question without the bother of asking him.

Practice paper 2

■ Read the questions below carefully. To guide your answer, remember to highlight the key words in the questions, then skim and scan the text to find the same or similar clues for your answers.

■ These questions are about the extract from *The Hobbit* by JRR Tolkien.

Write your answers on a separate sheet of paper.

1. Hobbits live in...
a) a nasty, dirty, wet hole
b) a dry, bare, sandy hole
c) [a hole] filled with the ends of worms and an oozy smell
d) a hobbit-hole, and that means comfort *(1 mark)*

2. The best rooms looked over...
a) his garden, and meadows beyond
b) his vegetable patch and flowerbeds
c) the town and surrounding houses
d) the boats on the river *(1 mark)*

3. Was the hobbit sociable? How do you know that? *(1 mark)*

4. Did every room have a view? How do you know that? *(1 mark)*

5. What do you think the author means when he says that Baggins was 'well-to-do'? *(2 marks)*

6. Do you think that Baggins spent much of his time in his home? How do you know that? *(2 marks)*

7. Had the Bagginses lived in the hill for many years? How do you know that? *(1 mark)*

8. What do you think Baggins might have enjoyed doing with his time? Why do you say that? *(3 marks)*

9. Describe what sort of person you think Baggins was. Why do you say that? *(3 marks)*

TOTAL

Practice paper 3

■ Read the following extract and remember to skim and scan for context clues to clarify unknown words; to predict what will happen next and to predict possible literal, inference and evaluation questions that you might be asked.

Oliver Twist
by Charles Dickens

Chapter VIII, page 47

By degrees the shutters were opened; the window-blinds were drawn up, and people began passing to and fro. Some few stopped to gaze at Oliver for a moment or two, or turned round to stare at him as they hurried by; but none relieved him, or troubled themselves to inquire how he came there. He had no heart to beg. And there he sat.

He had been crouching on the step for some time, wondering at the great number of public-houses (every other house in Barnet was a tavern, large or small); gazing listlessly at the coaches as they passed through, and thinking how strange it seemed that they could do, with ease, in a few hours, what it had taken him a whole week of courage and determination beyond his years to accomplish; when he was roused by observing that a boy, who had passed him carelessly some minutes before, had returned, and was now surveying him most earnestly from the opposite side of the way. He took little heed of this at first; but the boy remained in the same attitude of close observation so long, that Oliver raised his head, and returned his steady look. Upon this, the boy crossed over, and, walking close up to Oliver, said 'Hello! My covey, what's the row?'

The boy who addressed this inquiry to the young wayfarer was about his own age, but one of the queerest-looking boys that Oliver had ever seen. He was snub-nosed, flat-browed, common-faced boy enough, and as dirty a juvenile as one would wish to see; but he had about him all the airs and manners of a man. He was short of his age, with rather bow-legs, and little, sharp, ugly eyes. His hat was stuck on the top of his head so lightly, that it threatened to fall off every moment – and would have done so very often, if the wearer had not had a knack of every now and then giving his head a sudden twitch, which brought it back to its old place again. He wore a man's coat, which reached nearly to his heels.

Practice paper 3

■ Read the questions below carefully. To guide your answer, remember to highlight the key words in the questions, then skim and scan the text to find the same or similar clues for your answers.
■ These questions are about the extract from *Oliver Twist* by Charles Dickens.

Write your answers on a separate sheet of paper.

1. Oliver crouched on the steps as people passed by and...
a) stared at them
b) waved at the coaches
c) gazed listlessly at the coaches
d) begged   *(1 mark)*

2. Every other house in Barnet was...
a) large
b) a tavern
c) a coach house
d) small   *(1 mark)*

3. What could the coaches do that took Oliver a whole week to accomplish?   *(1 mark)*

4. Was Oliver in awe of the number of public houses in Barnet? Why do you say that?   *(1 mark)*

5. What do you think Charles Dickens meant when he said it had taken Oliver 'courage and determination beyond his years'?   *(2 marks)*

6. What was it about the boy that first caught Oliver's attention?
                                                                    (2 marks)

7. What do you think Oliver thought of the boy? Why do you say that?
                                                                    (3 marks)

8. How do you think Oliver was feeling as he sat on the steps that morning?   *(3 marks)*

TOTAL

QUICK FIX FOR YEAR 6: COMPREHENSION

Practice paper 4

■ Read the following non-fiction extract from a magazine, remembering to skim and scan for context clues to clarify unknown words; to predict what will happen next and to predict possible literal, inference and evaluation questions that you maight be asked.

COPTER CAMERA
The 'heligimbal' has revolutionised wildlife filming

The heligimbal is a high-definition, long-lens camera that can swivel through 360 degrees. Its body is about 50cm in diameter, and is the shape of an oversized basketball, housed in a protective cover and suspended beneath the nose of a helicopter.

ASK THE EXPERT

Michael Kelem, the Hollywood cameraman who used the heligimbal for Planet Earth, says he'd rather film wildlife than feature films.

How has the heligimbal changed wildlife filming?
It provides a steady platform in the sky. Even at 300m the shot is stable because of the gyroscopes. To get close enough to film natural behaviour you used to have to film from the ground, but from the helicopter you can choose where you film from and follow the action. It's expensive, though. That's part of the reason why it's not been used for wildlife filming before.

What's the main difference between shooting wildlife and feature films?
You need massively improved concentration! In feature films you do a shot which maybe lasts a minute, then you rest. But when I filmed wild dogs hunting in the Okavango, for example, they were difficult to follow, because they blended into the scenery and dodged between trees. I couldn't take my eye off the monitor for a full 40-minute take. That was the most tiring work I've ever done.

What tricks do you use in feature films that you applied to filming wildlife?
No matter how carefully you script something, in the air you have to change the shot as needs be. This flexibility helped me when filming wildlife, because you have to adapt to the action.

What was the highlight of Planet Earth for you?
Filming wolves hunting caribou in the Arctic, because we got five hunts within a couple of hours. Apparently that never happens. And shooting Mount Everest was pretty spectacular.

What would you rather work with – wildlife or Hollywood divas?
The work ethic of wildlife and the Hollywood diva are very similar – they work hard for a couple of hours in the morning, hunt and eat their prey (whether that's a caribou or a submissive director) and then take the afternoon off. The catering is better in Hollywood, but it can be a sick industry. The people in wildlife are more down to Earth.

BBC Focus Magazine, March 2006

Practice paper 4

■ Read the questions below carefully. To guide your answer, remember to highlight the key words in the questions, then skim and scan the text to find the same or similar clues for your answers.

■ These questions are about the *BBC Focus* non-fiction magazine article about wildlife filming.

Write your answers on a separate sheet of paper.

1. What is a heligimbal?
a) A long-lens camera
b) A wild animal
c) A digital camera
d) A helicopter   *(1 mark)*

2. What measures have been taken to prevent camera damage during flight?
a) It is kept inside the helicopter.
b) It is suspended beneath the nose of the helicopter.
c) It can swivel through 360 degrees.
d) It has a protective cover.   *(1 mark)*

3. What are the advantages and disadvantages of using a heligimbal?
                          (2 marks)

4. How does filming wildlife compare to shooting a feature film?   *(2 marks)*

5. How do you think being flexible makes wildlife filming more successful?
                          (3 marks)

6. What was the most spectacular part of filming for Michael?   *(1 mark)*

7. Explain what you would like most about either wildlife or feature filming, and why.   *(3 marks)*

TOTAL

Name _____

Practice paper 5

■ Read the following non-fiction extract from a newspaper, remembering to skim and scan for context clues to clarify unknown words; to predict what will happen next and to predict possible literal, inference and evaluation questions that you might be asked.

Daily Mail, Thursday March 30, 2006

Chimps make toddlers look chumps at solving puzzles

PARENTS often marvel at how quickly their children seem to pick up new tricks.

So they may be dismayed to learn that compared to young chimpanzees, toddlers can appear a little dim.

Research has shown that while children blindly copy adults, chimps try to find a way to do things better. The result is that the animals often outdo their human cousins at finding the answer to problems.

Scientists from St. Andrews University looked at how a group of chimps aged from two to six and a group of children aged between three and four fared when presented with a puzzle.

They were given a dark-coloured box held closed by a variety of bolts and doors. Deep inside lay either a sticker or piece of food.

The children and chimps were given a demonstration of how to open the box and get their reward. The scientists then watched as the groups tried it themselves. Initially, both the children and chimps imitated the demonstrator's actions.

The scientists then swapped the dark box for a transparent one, which made it easier to work out the quickest and best way to get to the reward.

The children continued to faithfully follow the technique they were shown – even if it was now clear there was an easier way to open the box. The chimps, however, pared down their actions, just doing those needed to quickly get inside.

The results suggested that while both chimps and children can imitate, chimps will work things out for themselves when they can. While the chimps' approach may appear more sensible, scientists say the children's attitude is more beneficial in the long-term. Researcher Professor Andrew Whiten told New Scientist magazine: 'Because humans have massive cultural complexity, children need to learn quickly how to do many things, and they can modify techniques later if need be.

Imitation is quicker because it provides a ready-made solution to the problem.'

It is also thought that humans make a point of tutoring children on the best way to do things – a trait not generally shared by chimps.

Text © 2006, Daily Mail

Practice paper 5

■ Read the questions below carefully. To guide your answer, remember to highlight the key words in the questions, then skim and scan the text to find the same or similar clues for your answers.

■ These questions are about the *Daily Mail* newspaper article, 'Chimps make toddlers look chumps at solving puzzles'.

Write your answers on a separate sheet of paper.

1. Parents often marvel at...
a) how quickly their children pick up new tricks
b) how children solve puzzles
c) how chimps solve puzzles
d) how quickly chimps pick up
e) new tricks   *(1 mark)*

2. What are the ages of the groups of chimps and children involved in the research? (Circle two options to give the correct answer).

    a) Children aged between 3 and 4   **b)** Chimps aged 2–6
    c) Children aged 3–14   **d)** Chimps aged 1–5
                                                          (1 mark)

3. Explain in your own words what the headline of the article means.
                                                            (2 marks)

4. How might parents react to finding out that chimpanzees can appear to be more intelligent than their small children?   *(1 mark)*

5. What's the difference between the way children and chimps solve problems?   *(1 mark)*

6. Who are the researchers and where do they come from?   *(1 mark)*

7. How do the chimpanzees respond more effectively in the tests?
                                                            (2 marks)

8. Who do you think enjoyed solving puzzles more, the children or the chimps? Why do you say that?   *(3 marks)*

TOTAL

Practice paper 6

■ Read the following extract, remembering to skim and scan for context clues to clarify unknown words; to predict what will happen next and to predict possible literal, inference and evaluation questions that you might be asked.

The Hitchhiker's Guide to the Galaxy
by Douglas Adams

CHAPTER 3

ON THIS PARTICULAR THURSDAY, something was moving quietly through the ionosphere many miles above the surface of the planet; several somethings in fact, several dozen huge yellow chunky slablike somethings, huge as office blocks, silent as birds. They soared with ease, baking in electromagnetic rays from the star Sol, biding their time, grouping, preparing.

The planet beneath them was almost perfectly oblivious of their presence, which was just how they wanted it for the moment. The huge yellow somethings went unnoticed at Goonhilly, they passed over Cape Canaveral without a blip. Woomera and Jodrell Bank looked straight through them – which was a pity because it was exactly the sort of thing they'd been looking for all these years.

The only place they registered at all was on a small black device called a Sub-Etha Sens-O-Matic which winked away quietly to itself. It nestled in the darkness inside a leather satchel which Ford Prefect habitually wore slung around his neck. The contents of Ford Prefect's satchel were quite interesting in fact and would have made any Earth physicist's eyes pop out of his head, which is why he always concealed them by keeping a couple of dog-eared scripts for plays he pretended he was auditioning for stuffed in the top. Besides the Sub-Etha Sens-O-Matic and the scripts he had an Electronic Thumb – a short squat black rod, smooth and matt with a couple of flat switches and dials at one end; he also had a device which looked rather like a largish electronic calculator. This had about a hundred tiny flat press buttons and a screen about four inches square on which any one of a million 'pages' could be summoned at a moment's notice. It looked insanely complicated, and this was one of the reasons why the snug plastic cover it fitted into had the words DON'T PANIC printed on it in large friendly letters.

Practice paper 6

■ Read the questions below carefully. To guide your answer, remember to highlight the key words in the questions, then skim and scan the text to find the same or similar clues for your answers.
■ These questions are about *The Hitchhikers Guide to the Galaxy* by Douglas Adams.

Write your answers on a separate sheet of paper.

1. Something was moving quietly through the ionosphere. Was it...?
a) electronic rays
b) birds
c) several dozen office blocks
d) huge yellow chunky slablike somethings   *(1 mark)*

2. As they soared with ease, were they...?
a) grouping
b) preparing food
c) backing into the starship Sol
d) flying saucers   *(1 mark)*

3. Was the planet *aware* of its visitors?   *(2 marks)*

4. Who do you think will be the first person to notice their presence? Why do you say that?   *(2 marks)*

5. Describe two ways that Ford Prefect hid the Sub-Etha Sens-O-Matic.
                                                               (2 marks)

6. Apart from the Sub-Etha Sens-O-Matic, what else did Ford Prefect's satchel contain?   *(3 marks)*

7. Why do you think it was necessary to print 'don't panic' in large friendly letters?   *(3 marks)*

TOTAL

Name _____

Practice paper 7

■ Read the following poem, remembering to skim and scan for context clues to clarify unknown words; to *predict* what will happen next and to *predict* possible *literal, inference and evaluation* questions that you might be asked.

Something Told the Wild Geese

Something told the wild geese
   It was time to go.
Though the field lay golden
   Something whispered 'Snow'.
Leaves were green and stirring,
   Berries, lustre-glossed,
But beneath warm feathers
   Something cautioned, 'Frost'.
All the sagging orchards
   Steamed with amber spice,
But each wild breast stiffened
   At remembered ice.
Something told the wild geese
   It was time to fly –
Summer sun was on their wings,
   Winter in their cry.

by Rachel Field

Practice paper 7

■ Read the questions below carefully. To guide your answer, remember to highlight the key words in the questions, then skim and scan the text to find the same or similar clues for your answers.

■ These questions are about the poem 'Something told the wild geese' by Rachel Field. Write your answers on a separate sheet of paper.

1. The geese were told that it was time to...
a) follow each other
b) fly
c) find food
d) go back
e) to the wild   *(1 mark)*

2. The geese were...
a) wild
b) lost
c) golden
d) cold   *(1 mark)*

3. What season do you think it is? How do you know that?   *(2 marks)*

4. How do we know that winter is coming?   *(2 marks)*

5. Explain what the poet means by 'the field lay golden'.   *(2 marks)*

6. Why do you think the poet chose to use the phrase 'all the sagging orchards'?   *(2 marks)*

7. What do you think it was that told the wild geese to go? Why do you say that?   *(3 marks)*

8. How do you think the geese felt about the winter coming? Explain why you say that.   *(3 marks)*

TOTAL

Name _____

Practice paper 8

■ Read the following extract remembering to skim and scan.

The Witches
by Roald Dahl

How To Recognise A Witch *(Pages 25-26)*

"Witches wear gloves even in the house. They only take them off when they go to bed."

"How do you know all this, Grandmamma?"

"Don't interrupt," she said. "Just take it all in. The second thing to remember is that a REAL WITCH is always bald."

"Bald?" I said.

"Bald as a boiled egg," my grandmother said.

I was shocked. There was something indecent about a bald woman. "Why are they bald, Grandmamma?"

"Don't ask me why," she snapped. "But you can take it from me that not a single hair grows on a witch's head."

"How horrid!"

"Disgusting," my grandmother said.

"If she's bald, she'll be easy to spot," I said.

"Not at all," my grandmother said. "A REAL WITCH always wears a wig to hide her baldness. She wears a first-class wig. And it is almost impossible to tell a really first-class wig from ordinary hair unless you give it a pull to see if it comes off."

"Then that's what I'll have to do," I said.

"Don't be foolish," my grandmother said. "You can't go round pulling at the hair of every lady you meet, even if she is wearing gloves. Just you try it and see what happens."

"So that doesn't help much either," I said.

"None of these things is any good on its own," my grandmother said. "It's only when you put them all together that they begin to make a little sense. Mind you," my grandmother went on, "these wigs do cause a rather serious problem for witches."

"What problem, Grandmamma?"

"They make the scalp itch most terribly," she said. "You see, when an actress wears a wig, or if you or I were to wear a wig, we would be putting it on over our own hair, but a witch has to put it straight on to her naked scalp. And the underneath of a wig is always very rough and scratchy. It sets up a frightful itch on the bald skin. It causes nasty sores on the head. Wig-rash, the witches call it. And it doesn't half itch."

"What other things must I look for to recognise a witch?" I asked.

Practice paper 8

■ Read the questions below carefully. To guide your answer, remember to highlight the key words in the questions, then skim and scan the text to find the same or similar clues to for your answers.

■ Think about the type of question you are answering. Is it a literal 'who, what, where' question, where the answer is 'right there' in the text? Is it an inference question that asks you to think and search and explain how you know the answer? Or is it an evaluation question that asks you to say what you think, or feel about the characters motives or actions – thoughts that the author might agree with?

■ These questions are about the extract from *The Witches* by Roald Dahl. Write your answers on a separate sheet of paper.

1. What do witches wear everywhere till bedtime?
a) seashell   **b)** glasses   **c)** a long nightdress   **d)** a black cloak and hat
e) gloves, even in the house   *(1 mark)*

2. A real witch needs a wig to hide her...
a) own hair   **b)** wig-rash   **c)** true   **d)** identity   **e)** baldness   *(1 mark)*

3. What appalled the boy and his grandmother about witches? How do you know that?   *(1 mark)*

4. Why is it not always possible to recognise a real witch? Give a detailed explanation.   *(1 mark)*

5. "Bald as a boiled egg..." Why do you think the author has chosen this simile to describe baldness?   *(2 marks)*

6. Name three ways that real witches differ from ordinary people. *(1 mark)*

7. Do you think the boy believes what his grandmother is telling him? Why do you say that?   *(2 marks)*

8. Which description in this passage do you think is the most effective and why?   *(2 marks)*

9. What genre do you think is represented by this style of writing? Explain why you say this.   *(3 marks)*

TOTAL

QUICK FIX FOR YEAR 6: COMPREHENSION

ANSWERS

PRACTICE PAPER 1:
Kasper in the Glitter by Philip Ridley

1. Jingo warned Kasper not to move.

2. Yes, I think Jingo's friend Knucklehead was careless because he had let the dogs into the kitchen before, having being told by Jingo not to do so 'a million times' already.

3. Kasper didn't want to move around in the kitchen because Jingo told him 'not to move' as the dogs were dangerous/he was 'too scared to move'/the dogs were 'sure to attack' him if he dropped the basket.

4. Yes, I think the dogs are dangerous because it says that they were snarling and had long, vicious sharp teeth/Jingo said they would be dangerous if Kasper didn't 'keep very, very still'.

5. No, I don't think that Kasper had visited Jingo and Knucklehead before because he had to be told 'not to move' and didn't know that the dogs might be let into the kitchen.

6. Answers will vary and need to relate to the text: Three reasons why I think the dogs were so aggressive are **a)** They could 'sense Jasper's anxiety' **b)** they were being territorial and Jasper was a stranger **c)** They were guard dogs who were normally kept outside.

PRACTICE PAPER 2:
The Hobbit by JRR Tolkien

1. d) Hobbits live in 'a hobbit-hole, and that means comfort'.

2. a) The best rooms looked over 'his garden and meadows beyond'.

3. Yes, the hobbit was sociable because 'he was fond of visitors'.

4. No, not every room had a view because the rooms on the left-hand side were the 'only ones to have windows'.

5. I think the author means by 'well-to-do' that Baggins was comfortably well off/wealthy/rich and respectable.

6. Yes, I think that Baggins spent much of his time at home because he enjoyed entertaining visitors/he had a very 'comfortable tunnel' with 'lots of rooms' and facilities/he liked to keep his home clean, e.g. kept his chairs polished.

7. Yes, the Baggins had lived in the hole for many years because it says they had lived there for 'time out of mind', which suggests that they had been there for so long that it was hard to remember a time when they had not lived there.

8. Answers will vary and need to relate to the text: I think that Baggins would have enjoyed spending most of his time inviting his friends to stay, because of his many bedrooms, where he would cook for them storing the food in his many pantries and serving the food in his various dining-rooms. I think he would spend much of his time making his own clothes and choosing what to wear for these house-parties, as he had 'whole rooms devoted to clothes' or spending time looking out of his windows at the views 'over his garden' and beyond.'

9. Answers will vary and need to relate to the text: I think Baggins was the sort of person who was house-proud, honest and decent because people considered him to be 'respectable'/ he was sociable because 'he was fond of visitors'/ he was rather predictable because 'you could tell' what he would say without bothering to ask him, and unexciting because he did nothing that was 'unexpected' and he 'never had any adventures'.

PRACTICE PAPER 3:
Oliver Twist by Charles Dickens

1.c) Oliver crouched on the steps as people passed by and 'gazed listlessly at the coaches'.

2.b) Every other house in Barnet was 'a tavern'.

3. The coaches could travel miles 'with ease' 'in just a few hours', compared with the 'whole week of courage and determination' that it had taken Oliver to travel the same distance on foot.

4. Yes, Oliver was in awe of the number of public-houses in Barnet because it says he 'wondered' at the great number where 'every other house in Barnet was a tavern'.

5. I think that when Charles Dickens said that it had taken Oliver 'courage and determination beyond his years' he meant that he had summoned the courage and determination of a much older, more experienced person.

6. The boy caught Oliver's attention because at first he carelessly passed by, then returned and stood 'earnestly' observing Oliver for a long time.

7. Answers will vary but need to relate to the text: I think Oliver thought that the boy was friendly and curious because he had made a point of coming over to talk to him, when others had passed him by, and that he was a fascinating but rather strange-looking person, because alongside being a dirty, short, bow-legged 'common-faced boy' wearing an outsized man's coat, he was also very confident with the 'airs and manners of a man'.

8. Answers will vary but need to relate to the text: I think Oliver was feeling emotionally drained after his long, difficult journey which had required so much courage and determination, and he was feeling quite in awe at the number of different sized taverns and by the busy people rushing by. He may also have felt rather lonely, lost and tired as he sat alone on the steps 'gazing listlessly' around the unknown town.

PRACTICE PAPER 4:
'Copter Camera', BBC Focus magazine

1.a) A heligimbal is a long-lens camera.

2.d) It has a protective cover.

3. The advantages of using a heligimbal is that 'it provides a steady platform', the 'shot' remains 'stable' 'even at 300m', you can 'choose where you film from' and 'you can follow the action' in a helicopter. The disadvantage is that it is expensive.

4. The difference between wildlife filming and shooting a feature film is that wildlife filming is often more 'tiring' and you need 'massively improved concentration' over periods of time as long as 40 minutes compared to shooting feature films where you do a shot that maybe only lasts a minute and then you rest.

5. I think that being flexible makes wildlife filming more successful because if you are working with animals in the wild anything can happen, so 'no matter how carefully you script something', you may have 'to change the shot' to 'adapt to the action'.

6. The most spectacular part of filming for Michael was when he filmed 'wolves hunting caribou in the Artic' and shooting 'Mount Everest'.

7. Answers will vary and must relate to the text: I would most like to film wildlife from the air using the heligimbal because you are able to have greater freedom with the shots than is probably the case with feature filming. Also I think it would be very exciting to film the unpredictable action above such amazing landscapes that comes with wildlife filming.

PRACTICE PAPER 5:
'Chimps make toddlers look chumps at solving puzzles', Daily Mail

1. a) Parents often marvel at how quickly their children pick up new tricks.

2. a) and **b)** Involved in the research are a group of chimps aged 2–6 and a group of children aged between 3 and 4.

3. I think the headline means that chimps make small children look unintelligent/dim/stupid at solving puzzles.

4. I think parents may be 'dismayed' to find out that chimpanzees can appear to be more intelligent than their children.

5. The difference between the way the children and chimps solve problems is that 'while children blindly copy adults', chimps try to find the 'quickest and best way to get to the reward'.

6. The researchers are scientists from St. Andrews University.

7. Chimps respond more effectively in the tests because they 'work things out for themselves when they can'.

8. Answers may vary and must relate to the text: I think that the chimps enjoyed solving the puzzles because they weren't concerned about failing the demonstrator's technique, and were rewarded for finding the quickest and easiest way on their own.

PRACTICE PAPER 6:
TheHitchhiker's Guide to the Galaxy by Douglas Adams

1. a) It was huge yellow chunky slablike somethings.

2. a) As they soared with ease they were grouping.

3. No, the planet was not aware of its visitors, it was 'oblivious'.

4. I think that the first person who will be aware of their presence will be Ford Prefect because 'the only place they registered at all' was on a small black device called a Sub-Etha Sens-O-Matic that he had with him.

5. Two ways that Ford Prefect had hidden the Sub-Etha Sens-O-Matic was a) in his leather satchel, b) concealed by a couple of playscripts.

6. Apart from the Sub-Etha Sens-O-Matic the other items that Ford Prefects satchel contained were an Electronic Thumb, another device that looked like an electronic calculator, and two playscripts.

7. Answers may vary and must relate to the text: I think that it was necessary to print 'don't panic' in large friendly letters to prevent a user from feeling intimidated by it and to feel confident about using it./I don't think that it helped that 'don't panic' was printed in large friendly letters on the case because it still didn't change the fact that it looked 'insanely complicated' to use .

PRACTICE PAPER 7:
'Something Told the Wild Geese' by Rachel Field

1. b) The geese were told that it was time to go.

2. a) The geese were wild.

3. I think the season is early autumn because the golden fields of corn and the orchard fruit are ready for harvesting, the fallen apples are rotting or the steam is more visible from them in the cooler autumn day.

4. We know that winter is coming because 'something whispers snow', the 'berries are lustre-glossed' and ripe, there is a hint of 'frost' in the air and 'winter' is in the bird's cry.

5. When the poet says that 'the field lay golden' she means it is full of ripened corn.

6. The poet uses the phrase 'all the sagging orchards' as a contrast between the plentiful food supplies in autumn and the bleak emptiness of the trees in winter.

7. I think it was a cold wind that told the geese to go because it 'whispered snow' (suggesting blowing and chilliness) and cautioned as if talking to the birds - warning them that frost was on the way.

8. I think the geese felt fearful ('each wild breast stiffened' and 'winter in their cry') when the chill in the air reminded them of the cold and ice ('remembered ice') so there was urgency in their flight, even though the 'summer sun was still on their wings'.

PRACTICE PAPER 8:
The Witches by Roald Dahl

1. e) The witches wore 'gloves even in the house'.

2. e) A real witch needs a wig to 'hide her baldness'

3. The boy and his grandmother were appalled that witches were bald because the boy thought it was 'indecent' and his grandmother said it was 'disgusting'.

4. It is not always possible to recognise a real witch because they wear quality wigs and it is 'almost impossible to tell a really first-class wig from ordinary hair'.

5. I think that the author has chosen the simile 'bald as a boiled egg' to describe baldness because it suggests a hairless head that is as pale, smooth and shiny as a boiled egg.

6. Three ways that real witches differ from ordinary people is that they are 'bald as a boiled egg', they often have 'wig-rash', and they wear gloves even in the house and only take them off when they go to bed.

7. Answers will vary but must relate to the text: No, I don't think the boy believes what his grandmother is telling him at one point, because he says 'how do you know all this, Grandmama?' Also he doesn't think that a witch could smell him when he'd just had a bath./ es, I think he does believe what she is telling him, because he is shocked about a witch's baldness and concerned to know what to look for to recognise a witch.

8. Answers will vary but must relate to the text.

9. I think that the genre represented by this text is humorous because Roald Dahl includes a number of very funny ideas 'like pulling the hair off every lady you meet'.